ABRAHAM & FAMILY

*New Insights into
the Patriarchal Narratives*

ABRAHAM & FAMILY

New Insights into the Patriarchal Narratives

Edited by Hershel Shanks

Lippman Bodoff

Philip R. Davies

Samuel Dresner

Carl D. Evans

Richard Elliott Friedman

Zefira Gitay

Larry R. Helyer

Robin M. Jensen

Jonathan Kirsch

Curt Leviant

Jack Miles

Jacob Milgrom

William R. Stegner

Gordon Tucker

Elie Wiesel

BIBLICAL ARCHAEOLOGY SOCIETY
WASHINGTON, D.C.

Library of Congress Cataloging-in-Publication Data
Abraham & Family: new insights into the patriarchal narratives/edited by Hershel Shanks
p. cm.

"Each [of the chapters in this book] was originally published
in Bible Review."—Front matter
Includes bibliographical references.
ISBN 1-880317-57-5 (paper)

1. Patriarchs (Bible) 2. Bible. O.T. Genesis—Criticism, interpretation, etc.
I. Shanks, Hershel. II. Bible review (Washington, D.C.)
BS573.A36 2000
222'.1106–dc21   00-058553

Design by AURAS Design, Silver Spring, MD
ISBN 1-880317-57-5

TABLE OF CONTENTS

ILLUSTRATIONS

COLOR PLATES

AUTHORS

LIPPMAN BODOFF, since his retirement in 1986 as assistant general counsel of AT&T Technologies, has devoted himself to Jewish studies. An associate editor of the scholarly journal *Judaism* for four years, his essays have appeared in numerous journals.

PHILIP R. DAVIES is professor of biblical studies at the University of Sheffield in England. He specializes in the Dead Sea Scrolls and ancient Israelite and Judean history. His publications include *The Damascus Covenant* (JSOT Press, 1992), *Qumran* (Eerdmans, 1982), *In Search of Ancient Israel* (JSOT, 1992) and *Whose Bible Is It Anyway?* (Sheffield Academic Press, 1995). His most recent book is *Scribes and Schools: The Canonization of the Hebrew Scriptures* (Westminster John Knox, 1998). He is a cofounder of Sheffield Academic Press and a consulting editor of *The Dictionary of Classical Hebrew* (Sheffield Academic Press, 1993-).

SAMUEL DRESNER, who died in May 2000, received his rabbinic ordination in 1951 and a doctorate in Hebrew letters in 1954 from the Jewish Theological Seminary, where he studied under Abraham Joshua Heschel. A visiting professor at JTS and an adjunct professor at Hebrew University and Spertus College, he wrote and edited books on Jewish thought and practice. His publications include *The Zaddik* and *World of a Hasidic Master: Levi Yitzhak of Berditchev*, both of which were reissued by Aronson in 1994, the same year he published *Rachel* (Fortress). He also coauthored *Abraham Joshua Heschel: Prophetic Witness* (with Edward K. Kaplan; Yale University Press, 1998).

CARL D. EVANS is an ordained elder of the United Methodist Church. He served as a pastor in his home state of Kansas for several years before joining academia. An associate professor of religious studies and department chair at the University of South Carolina, Evans has published widely in scholarly journals and is coeditor of *Scripture in Context:*

Essays on the Comparative Method (with William B. Hallo and John B. White; Pickwick, 1980). He is currently working on a book about religious and cultural diversity in ancient Judah. He is an active worker in ecumenical and interfaith organizations.

RICHARD ELLIOTT FRIEDMAN is professor of Hebrew and comparative literature and the Katzin Professor of Jewish Civilization at the University of California, San Diego. His popular *Who Wrote the Bible?* (Prentice Hall, 1987) was selected by the Book-of-the-Month Club and the Quality Paperback Book Club and has been published in eight foreign editions. *The Disappearance of God* (Little Brown, 1995), published in paperback as *The Hidden Face of God* (HarperSanFrancisco, 1997), was a Publishers Weekly Best Book of 1998. His most recent book is *Commentary on the Torah* (HarperSanFrancisco, 2000).

ZEFIRA GITAY was born in Israel and studied archaeology and Jewish history at Hebrew University. She has participated in several archaeological excavations in Israel and was curator at the Prehistoric Museum in Haifa. Her doctoral studies at Emory University focused on Renaissance art history. The author of *The Artist as a Biblical Commentator,* she specializes in art and the Bible.

LARRY R. HELYER is professor of biblical studies at Taylor University in Upland, Indiana. He is the author of *Yesterday, Today and Forever: The Continuing Relevance of the Old Testament* (Sheffield Publications, 1996) and *Jewish Literature of the Second Temple Period* (InterVarsity, forthcoming). He is currently translating 2 Samuel for the new Holman Christian Standard Bible, to be published in 2003.

ROBIN M. JENSEN is associate professor of the history of Christianity at Andover Newton Theological School. She specializes in the literature of the early church and in the history of worship and liturgy. Her most recent book, *Understanding Early Christian Art* (Routledge, 2000), reflects her expertise in the history of Christian art and architecture. Her other scholarly interests include the history of worship, the social context of Christianity, regional and cultural diversity in early Christian movements, and the historical interactions of Muslims, Christians and Jews. She is director of Andover Newton's program in theology and the arts.

JONATHAN KIRSCH is an author, a book critic for *The Los Angeles Times* and an attorney specializing in publishing law and other intellectual property matters. His most recent book is *King David: The Real Life of the Man Who Ruled Israel* (Ballantine, 2000). He is also the author of *Moses: A Life* (Ballantine, 1998), a definitive but "unauthorized" biography, and *The Harlot by the Side of the Road: Forbidden Tales of the Bible* (Ballantine, 1997).

CURT LEVIANT lectures widely on various aspects of Hebrew and Yiddish literature. A recipient of fellowships from the National Endowment for the Humanities, the National Endowment for the Arts, the Rockefeller Foundation and the Jerusalem Foundation, his publications include *Masterpieces of Hebrew Literature: A Treasury of 2000 Years of Jewish Creativity*; translations from Yiddish of the works of Sholom Aleichem, Chaim Grade and Abraham Reisen; and four critically acclaimed novels, *The Yemenite Girl, Passion in the Desert, The Man Who Thought He Was Messiah, Partita in Venice*, and his latest novel, *Diary of an Adulterous Woman*.

JACK MILES is the author of the Pulitzer Prize-winning *God: A Biography* (Knopf, 1995), which has been translated into 15 languages. He is senior adviser to the president of the J. Paul Getty Trust in Los Angeles. His writing has appeared in many publications, including the *New York Times*, the *Washington Post* and the *Los Angeles Times*, where he served as a book editor and member of the editorial board.

JACOB MILGROM is professor emeritus of Hebrew and Bible at the University of California at Berkeley, where he founded the Jewish studies program. He is the recipient of the Rabbi Solomon

Goldman Award for Literary Creativity and was awarded a Guggenheim Fellowship to study the Temple Scroll, the largest of the Dead Sea Scrolls. In addition, he is a Fulbright fellow, a fellow of the Biblical Colloquium, a fellow of the Advanced Institute at Hebrew University and a senior fellow of the Albright Institute of Archaeological Studies, in Jerusalem. He is the author of more than 200 scholarly articles, and his books include the three-volume commentary *Leviticus* in the Anchor Bible series (Doubleday, 1991-2000). He now resides in Jerusalem.

HERSHEL SHANKS is the founder, editor and publisher of *Biblical Archaeology Review*, *Archaeology Odyssey* and *Bible Review*. He is the author of *The Mystery and Meaning of the Dead Sea Scrolls* (Random House, 1998), *Jerusalem: An Archaeological Biography* (Random House, 1995), *The City of David* (Biblical Archaeology Society, 1973), *Judaism in Stone: The Archaeology of Ancient Synagogues* (Biblical Archaeology Society and Harper & Row, 1979) and other books. A graduate of Harvard Law School, he has also published widely on legal topics.

WILLIAM R. STEGNER, an ordained elder in the United Methodist Church, is professor emeritus of New Testament at Garrett Evangelical Theological Seminary. He was president of the Chicago Society of Biblical Research from 1985 to 1986 and now serves on the editorial board of the society's journal, *Biblical Research*, and the board of reference for the *Asbury Theological Journal*. His published works include *An Introduction to the Parables Through Programmed Instruction* (University Press of America, 1977), *Forms in the Gospels—The Pronouncement Story* (Abingdon, 1970) and *Narrative Theology in Early Jewish Christianity* (Westminster John Knox, 1989).

GORDON TUCKER is assistant professor of Jewish philosophy at the Jewish Theological Seminary. He serves on the Committee on Jewish Law and Standards of the Rabbinical Assembly, the national organization of

Conservative rabbis. He has also served as a White House fellow and a special assistant to U.S. Attorney General Benjamin Civiletti.

ELIE WIESEL, university professor and Andrew W. Mellon Professor in the Humanities at Boston University, is a world-renowned author and speaker. His personal experience of the Holocaust has led him to use his talents as an author, a teacher and a storyteller to defend human rights and peace throughout the world. His more than 40 books have won numerous awards; his first publication, *La Nuit* (*Night*), has been translated into more than 25 languages and has sold millions of copies. He was awarded the Nobel Peace Prize in 1986. Two volumes of his memoirs have been published by Knopf: *All Rivers Run to the Sea—Memoirs* (1995) and *And the Sea Is Never Full* (1999).

ACKNOWLEDGMENTS

First among the people to whom this book owes its existence are the authors. The 15 scholars whose articles are reprinted here graciously agreed to this second publication of their work in the expectation that it would enable us to continue our conversation with the biblical text.

But there are others without whom the book would not have taken shape. The Biblical Archaeology Society staff members who worked on this project in addition to their already substantial responsibilities helped select the articles and illustrations that appear in this book and saw it through the many steps from idea to finished product. I especially want to thank Susan Hunt, special projects editor, who oversaw this project from beginning to end. Our design director, Rob Sugar, created the book's design with assistance from Robin Cather and David Fox, and then turned it over to the capable hands of Frank Sheehan. Sara Murphy and Lauren Krause dealt with the complicated stages of production.

Assistant editor Devra Wexler cast a careful eye on all the details of copyediting. Bonnie Mullin and Lyn Taecker provided editorial assistance. Managing editors Steven Feldman and Molly Dewsnap Meinhardt supervised the editorial work. Bridget Young, our executive director, contributed her unfailing encouragement and support throughout this enterprise.

Thanks to one and all.

Hershel Shanks

INTRODUCTION

This is a book for Bible Study Groups—and others, too, of course. But it was the Bible Study Group that I had in mind when this project was conceived.

I think I know the Bible Study Group. I feel with it. I understand it. For it was a Bible Study Group that got me started in my late 20s. Although I had gone to Sunday School, I had never really studied the Bible. I had been to college, I had taken a master's degree and even had a law degree. I was a lawyer with the United States Department of Justice. But I had never read—let alone taken a course on—the Bible.

Frankly, I was curious. At the time, some friends and I had an informal play-reading group that we jocularly called the Thursday Evening Legal Discussion and Play-reading Group. We were all single, and the men, although not the women, were lawyers (as was common in those days, only three of the 500 people in my law school class were women). I suggested we start another group that would meet every other Sunday evening to discuss the Bible. And that was how it all started: I am, so to speak, the child of this Bible Study Group.

Gradually the various members began to develop more specialized interests in our joint endeavor—theology, rabbinic exegesis, textual criticism, Marxist interpretation, etc. Each member brought a different perspective to the discussion. Mine happened to be archaeology. But we all shared a literary interest. We all felt the power of the text. We realized the depths of the characters described in the pages. We recognized the myriad meanings embedded in every line. As the Talmud, that arcane repository of rabbinical learning, puts it, "Turn it and turn it again, for everything is in it" (Mishnah, *Pirkei Avot* 5:22).

After nearly 40 years, the members of my Bible Study Group have all gone their own ways, yet we remain good friends and still meet for a discussion once a year.

Of course the primary text for any Bible Study Group is the Bible itself. And I must confess that in my own Bible Study Group, a number of people felt that the Bible alone was sufficient. They didn't feel the need to read any secondary texts. They had *quite* enough to say just from reading the Bible. If you note a little sarcasm in my tone at this point, you are reading me accurately. On the one hand, it *is* important not to stray too far from the text. But it is also important not to be intimidated by it. The text is legitimately the father to your own ideas. Don't be afraid to express them. Dare to wrestle with the text. And don't worry about being shown to be wrong—that happens to all of us.

Traditional Jewish study requires a partner, a *havruta*. One does not study alone. Together the pair reads the text, and each person explains what meaning he or she finds there. Together, you question, you argue, you concede, you build one idea upon another. You learn. One writer coined the word "Godwrestling," which could apply here. In a sense, both Bible Study Groups and this book are expansions of the idea of the learning pair. With this volume, you invite to your Bible Study Group some of the greatest modern minds that have analyzed the biblical text.

We are all limited in our perceptions. It can be both exciting and stimulating to see what others have seen in these texts. Secondary literature, if it is good, can be a *havruta*, another member of the group. This is both the strength and the limitation of secondary literature. It doesn't have the standing we give the biblical text, but it can be part of the conversation—it can be questioned, argued with, sometimes accepted, but it will almost always be a catalyst for further thought.

We had this in mind when we assembled the various contributions to this book. They are by no means presented as the final word. They are here to raise questions in *your* mind, to stimulate *your* thoughts about the text, to be accepted—or rejected—by *you*. Some of the chapters are daring, some are traditional, some are imaginative, but all are insightful, in one way or another, and all are fun to read and to talk about. Contending with them, you will find that they deepen your engagement with the biblical text.

Of course, this book is not intended *only* for Bible Study Groups. It will be used in Sunday Schools, in church and synagogue classes, in universities and colleges, in seminaries and graduate schools. Preachers will also find it thought-provoking and inspiring.

There is something comforting about knowing this. We are all engaged in our very different ways in attempting to plumb the depths of a book that has played such a formative role in shaping Western civilization—and in connecting us to the divine, however we may understand that concept.

The chapters in this book comment and reflect on the stories about Abraham and his family—the patriarchs and matriarchs of Israel and their children. Each was originally published as an article in *Bible Review*, the Biblical Archaeology Society's nondenominational Bible magazine. Now they can become part of *your* discussion, part of your Godwrestling.

Hershel Shanks
September 2000
Washington, D.C.

I

ABRAHAM AND ISAAC

After these things God tested Abraham. He said
to him, "Abraham!" And he said, "Here I am."
He said, "Take your son, your only son Isaac,
whom you love, and go to the land of Moriah,
and offer him there as a burnt offering on one
of the mountains that I shall show you."

GENESIS 22:1-2

1

THE BINDING OR SACRIFICE OF ISAAC

How Jews and Christians See Differently

ROBIN M. JENSEN

The *Akedah* (ah-kay-DAH), or binding of Isaac, is one of the most powerful narratives in the Hebrew Bible. For nearly 2,000 years, however, it has been read somewhat differently by Jews and Christians. It is even portrayed differently in the pictures they make. For most Christians, the Hebrew word *akedah* is unfamiliar; more often than not, they will refer to the episode as the sacrifice of Isaac rather than the binding of Isaac.

Yet, as we shall see, at various times Christians and Jews were aware of each other's interpretation of the story.

According to the narrative in Genesis 22:2-18, God, without any warning, commands Abraham to sacrifice his beloved son as a burnt offering. Father and son travel three days to Moriah, the place of sacrifice, where they build an altar. Abraham binds Isaac, lays him on the firewood and raises his knife to slay him. At the last moment, however, an angel calls out to Abraham to do no harm to the lad, and a ram caught in a nearby thicket is substituted for Isaac.

In Judaism and Christianity (as well as Islam), Abraham is the paradigm of the man of faith, put to the ultimate test and found to be steadfast. Isaac, however, is variously interpreted according to time and tradition. In Islam, the son is unidentified and could have been Ishmael (Abraham's son by Hagar and the ancestor of the Arabs) instead of Isaac, thus extending God's covenant to the Arab peoples. In Jewish literature around the turn of the era, Isaac is portrayed as the prototype of the voluntary and joyful martyr, willing to go bravely to his death. The first-century C.E. Jewish historian Flavius Josephus describes Isaac as a 25-year-old who rushes to the altar, knowing that he is to be the victim.[1] According to this portrayal, in future times of distress, God will remember Isaac's binding, the *Akedah*, and heed the prayers of the Jewish people for deliverance from enemies. As the text says, "Because you have done this ... I will bestow my blessing upon you and make your descendants as numerous as the stars of heaven and the sands on the seashore" (Genesis 22:16-17). That is why the shofar, the ram's horn, is blown at Rosh Hashanah, to remind God of the *Akedah* and his promise: The shofar represents the horn of the ram that was substituted for Isaac.[2]

The Roman destruction of the Jerusalem Temple in 70 C.E. may have stimulated a profound new understanding of the *Akedah* in Jewish tradition. Since sacrifices could no longer be offered at the Temple, Isaac became the archetypal sacrifice, a kind of substitute for the now-defunct sacrificial system of the Temple. In Jewish tradition, until the destruction of the Temple, the episode was referred to as the "offering" of Isaac; after the destruction it was called the "binding" of Isaac, a reference to the tying of a lamb's feet in the days when this sacrifice was carried out at the Temple in Jerusalem. After the Temple's destruction, the word *akedah* was used to show that Isaac's offering and/or death was a vicarious atonement that was perfected and complete in itself; the former Temple offering was only a memorial to this archetypal sacrifice.[3]

In later rabbinic collections, Isaac is portrayed as an adult of 37 years, fully aware of what is going to happen to him. He not only accepts the role he is to play, but begs Abraham to bind him lest he struggle in fear, thus invalidating the sacrifice.[4] The Jerusalem Talmud summarizes the tradition that Isaac's release is the equivalent of all Israel's release. Abraham received from God, as a reward for his obedience, God's own future intercession for Isaac's descendants when they should fall into sin. Remembering the *Akedah*, God will suppress his wrath and have mercy on his people.[5]

According to the Genesis story, Isaac's sacrifice was interrupted and the ram substituted. However, several ancient traditions refer to Isaac's ashes or blood; some accounts even say that Isaac actually died and was revived.[6] Does Genesis itself hint at this? After God tells Abraham that, because of what he has done, his descendants will be like the stars of the heaven and the sands of the sea, "Abraham then returned to his servants, and they departed together for Beer-sheba" (Genesis 22:19). Why no mention of Isaac? What happened to him? Was there another version of the story with a different ending? In any event, in all these traditions Isaac's ashes are the symbol of his merit, and the *Akedah* is the fulfilled expiatory sacrifice.[7]

To resolve the seeming conflict between the tradition that he was sacrificed and the text that says a ram was substituted, later Jewish sages suggested that Isaac was laid upon the altar after the wood was kindled (in accordance with priestly law [Leviticus 1:7-8]). Although the angel prevented Abraham from slaying his son, Isaac was burned to death and his ashes cast on Moriah.[8] Moriah, in Jewish tradition, is the Temple Mount, where the Temple was later built and where sacrifices were offered in commemoration of the *Akedah*.

Christians, on the other hand, have from earliest times understood Isaac as a prefiguration of Christ, the beloved son offered as the

5

expiatory sacrifice for the people's sin. The textual parallels between Jesus and Isaac are striking. Isaac, like Jesus, was miraculously conceived. (Sarah, Isaac's mother, was 90 years old when she bore Isaac and had been barren all her life; Abraham was 100 [Genesis 17:17].) Isaac was his father's beloved son. Isaac carried the wood for his own sacrifice (Genesis 22:6), just as Christ carried his own cross. The journey to Moriah took three days, parallel to the three days Jesus spent in the tomb before his resurrection. And of course Jesus did Isaac one better: Isaac was not sacrificed; Jesus was.

Although these parallels are not explicitly drawn in the New Testament, later Christian exegetes made them quite specifically. Paul may even have intended his audience to make the connection when he described God as "He who did not withhold his own Son, but gave him up for all of us" (Romans 8:32).[9]

Very early in post-New Testament Christian literature, the story of Abraham's offering of Isaac becomes the "old covenant" counterpart of and paradigm for God's sacrifice of his own son on Calvary. The explicit connection occurs first in the Epistle of Barnabas, which is usually dated to the early second century. Some scholars have suggested that Barnabas, who was possibly a converted Jew familiar with early *Akedah midrashim*,* preached an Easter sermon that directly compared the atonement in the *Akedah* to Christ's atoning death, saying "not Isaac, but Jesus takes the place of the sacrifice."[10] This challenge was met with a direct response as the rabbis developed their own Passover atonement theology.[11] The rabbis, aware of the Christian typological interpretation of Isaac's sacrifice, developed the *Akedah* tradition in which the word *akedah* was interpreted to refer to the tying of the lamb's feet in a *tamid* sacrifice, the twice-a-day burnt offering at the Temple when it still stood.

---

*Midrash (plural, *midrashim*) designates a genre of rabbinic literature that dates roughly from 400 to 1550 C.E. The term refers to a nonliteral elaboration of a biblical text, often for homiletic purposes.

An early church father, Melito of Sardis, noted the parallels between Isaac and Christ but stressed that while Christ suffered and died, Isaac was released from his bonds.[12]

Irenaeus, Tertullian, Clement and Origen also cited the Isaac-Christ parallels. Tertullian saw the firewood Isaac carried as a figure of the cross and emphasized Christ's self-sacrifice: "Isaac, being led by his father to be a victim, and carrying himself the firewood, at that moment was a figure of Christ's death, submitting himself to his father as a victim and lugging the [fire]wood of his own passion."[13]

This interpretive motif continued through the fourth and fifth centuries with Ambrose, John Chrysostom, Theodoret and Augustine.[14] Perhaps the most significant use of the Isaac–Christ typology was in the liturgy of the church. The story of Isaac's sacrifice was read during the Easter vigil service in Jerusalem, and perhaps also in Milan, no later than the last half of the fourth century.[15]

As noted earlier, Jewish tradition identified Moriah, the site of the *Akedah*, as the Temple Mount, where the Temple of the Lord was later built. Christians, on the other hand, conflated Moriah with Calvary, the site of Jesus' sacrifice on the cross. By the end of the sixth century the common identity had been accepted. In his famous travel account, the anonymous writer known only as the Piacenza Pilgrim gave the following description of Golgotha: "You can see the place where [Jesus] was crucified, and on the actual rock there is a blood-stain. Beside this is the altar of Abraham, which is where he intended to offer Isaac, and where Melchizedek offered sacrifice."[16] Eventually a chapel dedicated to Abraham was built there.

That the rabbis were aware of the use to which their *Akedah* story had been put by the Christians is clear. In refutation one of them wrote:

How foolish is the heart of the deceivers who say the Holy One, Blessed Be He, has a son. If in the case of Abraham's son, when He saw that he was ready to slay him, He could not bear to look on as

7

He was in anguish, but on the contrary commanded, "Do not lay your hand on the lad"; had He a son, would He have abandoned him? Would He have turned the world upside down and reduced it to "a formless void" [*tohu ve-vohu*, the state of the universe before creation (Genesis 1:2)]?[17]

A careful look at Jewish and Christian depictions of the story and their settings reveals how they reflect the different religious traditions they represent.

The sacrifice of Isaac was one of the most popular scenes in early Christian art. From the Constantinian era (beginning in 312 C.E.) until the end of the sixth century, there remain at least 22 catacomb frescoes, approximately 90 sarcophagus reliefs, several important mosaics and dozens of smaller objects, including ivory pyxides, glasses, lamps and bowls, depicting the sacrifice of Isaac. This places it up there with images of Jonah, Noah, Moses and Daniel in popularity, making the sacrifice of Isaac a central theme of early Byzantine art.[18]

The two most significant Jewish depictions of the *Akedah* are in ancient synagogues, one in the third-century C.E. synagogue at Dura-Europos in modern Syria, where it is portrayed in a painting on dry plaster above the Torah niche, and the other in the sixth-century C.E. synagogue at Beth Alpha in Israel, where it is portrayed in a mosaic pavement.

Neither of these two Jewish examples comes from an urban center, and their style resembles folk art rather than high art. In the Beth Alpha mosaic (plate 1, p. 79), Abraham and Isaac are identified in Hebrew. The hand of God extends from heaven to prevent Abraham from proceeding. Below the hand are the Hebrew words "Lay not [your hand]." Next to the ram are the words "Behold a ram."

In the Dura-Europos synagogue, the *Akedah* scene shares the special panel above the Torah niche with a depiction of the Temple, as well as specifically Jewish symbols, including a menorah and a palm branch (*lulav*) and citron (*etrog*), both used on the festival of Sukkot. These objects also appear on a floor panel in the Beth Alpha synagogue.

Christian depictions of the sacrifice of Isaac, in contrast to the surviving Jewish images of the scene, appear most frequently in the artistic programs of tombs and sarcophagi. In the Roman catacombs, the sacrifice of Isaac appears near the raising of Lazarus (John 11:43-44); the story of Jonah (who returned from the belly of the fish after three days [Jonah 1:17], just as Jesus emerged from the tomb after three days); the healing of the paralytic (John 5:8-9); and the miracle of the three youths who emerged from the fiery furnace unsinged (Daniel 3:24-26). This juxtaposition sends a message of deliverance from illness and death, symbolized in part by Isaac, who was delivered by God. On two well-known sarcophagi—one from the Vatican Museum and the other the famous Junius Bassus sarcophagus in the Treasury of St. Peter's (also a part of the Vatican Museum)— the sacrifice of Isaac is balanced by scenes from the arrest and trial of Jesus, as if to emphasize the sacrifice of Isaac as a metaphor for the vicarious and atoning sacrifice of Christ.

In a fresco from the Priscilla catacomb in Rome (plate 2, p. 79), Isaac carries his own firewood. Is this because the artist had been influenced by Christian writers like Tertullian, who stressed the parallel between Isaac carrying the wood and Jesus carrying the cross? Or is it that the artist was simply faithfully portraying what he read in the biblical text?

In several Christian images, such as the mid-sixth-century mosaics in the Church of San Vitale in Ravenna, the sacrifice of Isaac is associated with the offerings of Abel (Genesis 4:4) and Melchizedek (Genesis 14:18-20). In San Vitale, a lunette in the sanctuary portrays a kind of Abraham cycle (plate 3, p. 80). To the left, Abraham and Sarah hear the announcement of Isaac's promised birth. Abraham offers a small calf on a platter to his three angelic visitors, who sit at a table on which three loaves are spread out. To the right, Abraham is about to sacrifice Isaac. Here Isaac is on the altar and Abraham's sword is aloft, but the hand of God has stayed it from striking. The ram substitute stands at

Abraham's feet. Directly across the sanctuary is a complementary lunette that depicts Abel and Melchizedek offering their sacrifices at an altar set with a chalice and two patens. Thus, the offering of Isaac is clearly identified with the sacrament of the Eucharist, which, for Christians, is the representation of Christ's sacrifice on the cross.

In Hebrews 5:5-10, Jesus is given a priestly lineage after the order of Melchizedek (just as in Luke 3:23-38 and Matthew 1:1-17 he is given a royal, i.e., Davidic, lineage). The portrayal of Melchizedek's offering is symbolic on at least two levels. First, Melchizedek prefigures Christ, who, in the person of the priest, is actually the celebrant of the Eucharist. Second, the offering foreshadows the sacrament and its elements.

The placement of the *Akedah* scene over the Torah niche in the Dura-Europos synagogue delivers a different message. Nearly two centuries after the destruction of the Temple, the *Akedah* scene may be telling us that the *Akedah*, rather than the Temple sacrifice, is the ultimate vicarious sacrifice and that the synagogue is the new locus of the faith—prayer and Torah reading have taken the place of sacrifice and Temple cult.[19]

Sometimes Jewish and Christian depictions bear similarities, if only because they portray the same text. In almost all the Christian catacomb frescoes of the sacrifice of Isaac and in the Beth Alpha synagogue mosaic of the *Akedah*, fires burn on the altar. Is this a reference to the Levitical regulation about setting the fire on the altar first, or does it allude to the midrash that Isaac was not killed by the knife but by the fire?[20]

In none of these instances is the image merely a biblical illustration. Each goes beyond the representation of the Genesis narrative and is meant to present a truth about the faith tradition itself. In a Christian context, whether in art or in literature, the sacrifice of Isaac directly refers to the salvation offered by the vicarious sacrifice of Christ on the cross. In a Jewish context, the image underscores

the importance of the *Akedah* as a meritorious act that can be shared with the people of Israel, reassuring the community that, although the Temple has been lost, Isaac's descendants are safe.
Reprinted from Bible Review, *October 1993.*

[1]Josephus, *Antiquities of the Jews* 20.12.1.

[2]See the discussion in Geza Vermes, *Scripture and Tradition in Judaism* (Leiden: Brill, 1961), pp. 206-208, 213; Erwin R. Goodenough, *Jewish Symbols in the Greco-Roman Period*, 13 vols. (Princeton, NJ: Princeton Univ. Press, 1953-1969), vol. 4, p. 173; Philip R. Davies and Bruce D. Chilton, "The Aqedah: A Revised Tradition History," *Catholic Biblical Quarterly* 40 (1978), pp. 534-535; and Shalom Spiegel, *The Last Trial*, trans. and introduction by Judah Goldin (New York: Behrman House, 1967; originally published in the *Alexander Marx Jubilee Volume* [New York: Jewish Theological Seminary, 1950]), pp. 471-547. According to Judah Goldin (Spiegel, *The Last Trial*, p. xix), the noun form of the Hebrew word *akedah* never occurs in scripture, and the verbal root occurs only seven times in the Bible in some form (six times as a passive participle). The verb as active—*wayaakod*, meaning "and he bound"—occurs only once in the Bible, in the story of Abraham's "binding" of Isaac (Genesis 22:9).

[3]See Spiegel, *The Last Trial.*

[4]*Genesis Rabbah* 56.4-8.

[5]See Jerusalem Talmud, *Ta'anit* 4.5; also *Pesiqta Rabbati* 39.

[6]See Babylonian Talmud, *Ta'anit* 16a; Jerusalem Talmud, *Ta'anit* 2.1 (on the ashes); *Mekhilta of R. Simeon ben Yohai*, on Exodus 16.2 (on the blood). Louis Ginzberg (*The Legends of the Jews*, 7 vols. [Philadelphia: Jewish Publication Society, 1909-1938], vol. 1, p. 281f., and vol. 5, p. 251) recounts the tradition that Isaac was also the name of the ram. See also the discussion in Hans Joachim Schoeps, "The Sacrifice of Isaac in Paul's Theology," *Journal of Biblical Literature* 65 (1946), p. 389; and Goodenough, *Jewish Symbols*, vol. 4, pp. 183-184.

[7]See discussions of dating and textual tradition in Davies and Chilton, "The Aqedah," pp. 537-546; and Spiegel, *The Last Trial*, pp. 28-49. Spiegel also cites late midrash on the *Shemoneh Esreh* prayer that describe Isaac's revival and asserts that it draws upon earlier *aggadah* (legends) concerning the burning and resurrection of Isaac.

[8]Spiegel, *The Last Trial*, pp. 35-37.

[9]See also Galatians 3:16 and 4:28 and Romans 9:7, as well as discussions in Nils Alstrup Dahl, *Jesus the Christ* (Minneapolis, MN: Fortress, 1991), pp. 138-140; and Robert J. Daly, "The Soteriological Significance of the Sacrifice of Isaac," *Catholic Biblical Quarterly* 39 (1977), pp. 45-75.

[10]Epistle of Barnabas 7.3.

[11]See Davies and Chilton, "The Aqedah," p. 538, citing L.W. Barnard, "Is the Epistle of Barnabas a Paschal Homily?" in *Studies in the Apostolic Fathers and Their Background* (Oxford: Basil Blackwell, 1966), p. 74.

[12]Melito of Sardis, *Excerptorum Libri Sex* 1-2, trans. in Isabel Speyert van Woerden, "The Iconography of the Sacrifice of Abraham," *Vigiliae Christianae* 15 (1961), p. 216.

[13]Tertullian, *Adversus Judaeos* 10, 6 (*Corpus Christianorum, Series Latina* [CCSL] 2.2 [1376]). See also *Adversus Judaeos* 13.20-22 (CCSL 2.2 [1388-1389]), in which Tertullian also refers to the bramble in which the ram was caught by the horns as a sign of the crown of thorns. See Irenaeus, *Adversus Haereses* 4.10.1.

[14]See Ambrose, *De Abraham* 1.8; John Chrysostom, *Homiliae in Genesin* 47.3; Theodoret, *Quaestiones in Genesin* 74; and Augustine, *De Civitate Dei* 16.32.

[15]See John Wilkinson, *Egeria's Travels* (Warminster, UK: Aris & Phillips, 1981), p. 253f.; and Thomas Talley, *The Origins of the Liturgical Year* (New York: Pueblo, 1986), p. 47f. Egeria does not give details of the vigil readings she attended when she was in Jerusalem, but liturgical scholars have argued that it is reasonably safe to assume the readings outlined in the Armenian lectionaries reflect a late-fourth-century tradition in Jerusalem. The readings include the Genesis stories of creation and the sacrifice of Isaac.

Talley argues that Egeria omitted the Easter vigil readings in Jerusalem because they were the ones she already knew and took for granted. Talley includes a table that shows fifth- to eighth-century documents that contain Easter vigil readings from Genesis 22.

[16]Piacenza Pilgrim, *Antonini Placentini Itinerarium* 19. See Wilkinson, *Jerusalem Pilgrims* (Warminster, UK: Aris & Phillips, 1977), p. 83. For other pilgrim accounts that place Abraham's altar on Calvary, see the discussion by Archer St. Clair, "The Iconography of the Great Berlin Pyxis," *Jahrbuch Berliner Museum* 20 (1978), p. 23f.

[17]Cited and dated by Spiegel, *The Last Trial*, p. 83, n. 26; also in Davies and Chilton, "The Aqedah," p. 539.

[18]This enumeration is based on a brief survey of the materials in the *Index of Christian Art* at Princeton University, as well as tables at the end of van Woerden, "Iconography," p. 243f. I should note here that I have found several mistakes and omissions in van Woerden's accounting, however. Other significant articles that analyze the Christian image of Abraham's sacrifice include Graydon Snyder, *Ante Pacem* (Macon, GA: Mercer Univ. Press, 1985), pp. 51-52; and Elizabeth S. Malbon, *The Iconography of the Sarcophagus of Junius Bassus* (Princeton, NJ: Princeton Univ. Press, 1990), p. 44f.

[19]See Joseph Gutmann, "Programmatic Painting in the Dura Synagogue," in *The Dura-Europos Synagogue*, ed. Gutmann (Missoula, MT: American Academy of Religion, 1973), pp. 147-150.

[20]See Spiegel, *The Last Trial*, pp. 34-40, in which he discusses midrash on the Shemoneh Esreh prayer concerning the burning up and resurrection of Isaac.

2

WHO'S TESTING WHOM

Was Abraham Really Ready to Kill His Son?

LIPPMAN BODOFF

In Jewish tradition, the Torah has 70—that is, many—facets. Its interpretations are inexhaustible. I would like to suggest a new interpretation of the *Akedah*, the binding of Isaac (Genesis 22), a story that has received as much "interpretation" as any in the Hebrew Bible.

The story of the *Akedah* has already been recounted in the preceding chapter. Briefly, God commands Abraham to slaughter his beloved son Isaac as a sacrifice to God. As Abraham is about to sacrifice the boy on the altar, an angel calls out to him to stop "because now I see that you are a God-fearing person and you would not withhold your son ... from me" (Genesis 22:12).

In the traditional understanding, God never intended Abraham to slaughter Isaac, because it was wrong—as we know from the beginning of the story, which speaks of God "testing" Abraham, and from the end of the story, when Abraham is told to desist. Abraham, on the other hand, out of fear of God, was willing to violate God's revealed moral law (the Noahide laws—Genesis 9:4-7) in faithfulness to God's command. Abraham passed the test.

The message of the *Akedah* is quite plainly that God does not want even his most God-fearing adherents to go so far as to murder in his name or even at his command. Indeed, the angel orders Abraham "not to do anything to [the boy]." Implicitly, we are being told, God will never ask for this kind of proof of loyalty or fear of God again. He only asked it of Abraham, the forefather of the Jewish people, to demonstrate Abraham's boundless fear of God.

Because Abraham is praised for being prepared to do what we may not do, and because God, the source of all morality, asked Abraham to do what no moral person before or since should ever contemplate, the *Akedah* has remained one of the most difficult texts to understand, justify and transmit to new generations.

I believe there is a countermessage in the text that exists in parallel with its traditional meaning, a simultaneous and necessary conceptual theological balance to the awesome mystery and the daunting problems of the traditional interpretation.

I believe that God was testing Abraham to see if he would remain loyal to God's moral law, but Abraham—who could not know this—was simultaneously testing God to see what kind of covenant and religion he, Abraham, was being asked to join.

After all, it was Abraham who found God, not the other way around. According to the midrash, "Until Abraham arrived, God reigned only over the heavens."[1] It was Abraham who "crowned" him God on earth, the God of man.[2] In these circumstances, Abraham not surprisingly had certain moral expectations—and perhaps even requirements—of the all-powerful God of the ordered universe, whose tradition as a God who abhorred violence and all immorality he had received and studied, and in whose name he was about to establish a new world religion.

In testing God, as it were, Abraham was, ultimately, testing himself. I have found God, he seems to be saying, and my tradition and experience have revealed him and made him known to me as an all-powerful, all-knowing, just and compassionate God. But I need to be sure that this is the God to whom I truly wish to dedicate myself and my progeny and my followers for all time. If the God I have found demands the same kind of immorality that I saw in my father's pagan society, I must be mistaken. I must look further. To obey such a God is not a moral advance at all. To paraphrase our sages: Better observance without God than God without observance.[3]

In short, Abraham wanted to see if God would stop him.

One may well ask, if this were the case, why didn't Abraham challenge God at the outset, when first commanded to sacrifice Isaac. Abraham had earlier done just that when God had told him of his plan to destroy Sodom and Gomorrah (Genesis 18:20-32).* We cannot justify Abraham's refusal to at least protest God's command that he kill Isaac on the grounds that prophets must *silently* obey whenever consulted or commanded by God. As shown above, the opposite is true when God's justice or compassion, and the morality of his commands, is at issue.

There is an alternative strategy, however—what Fania Fénelon called in her moving Holocaust memoir, "playing for time."[4] I do not believe Abraham ever intended to kill Isaac. He was obviously terribly concerned that God had commanded him to do so. However, those who seek simultaneously to obey their superiors—whom they admire, respect and sometimes fear—*and* give their superiors a

---

*This is in contrast to Noah, whom our sages criticize for not speaking up when God announced his plan to destroy the world by the Flood. Moses, too, was told about God's plan to destroy the Jewish people and start a new nation from Moses' progeny, after the sin of the golden calf (Exodus 32:1-14), and he is praised by our sages because he objected. In Jewish tradition, a prophet's conscientious objection to a divine plan or order is praiseworthy; in Jewish law, a prophet may only follow divine commands to violate God's law if his purpose is to protect the law. (See Responsum No. 652 of Radbaz, Rabbi David ibn Zimra of Egypt and Palestine, renowned 16th-century halakhic interpreter.)

IN THE BARREN ROCKY LANDSCAPE created by George Segal (1924-2000) for his sculpture The Sacrifice of Isaac, *Abraham, knife in hand, stands over Isaac and hesitates, as if giving God one last chance to rescind his command to "take your son, your only son Isaac, whom you love ... and offer him ... as a burnt offering" (Genesis 22:2). Author Lippman Bodoff suggests that Abraham is testing God by playing for time and waiting for the angel's voice, the hand of God and the sacrificial ram—harbingers of Isaac's eventual reprieve that are absent from this stark scene.*

chance to change their minds about what seems to be an unwise or immoral idea, rarely challenge the idea head on or rush to execute it. They act, but they're waiting and hoping. Time is an ally.

The matter may be compared to a father who asks his son to violate a religious commandment. The child does not know whether his father is testing his obedience to the law—which requires him to resist his father and observe the commandment—or his love (and fear) of his parent. The child can protest, showing disrespect and causing the parent anguish, or make the preparations to do what the parent has requested, seeming to go along, hoping that when the time comes the parent will never let the child take the last step.

This is precisely what the text tells us that Abraham did.[5] He acted promptly but deliberately. He conceived of the task that he was given as comprising numerous tasks, or steps. At each one he stopped, waiting to see whether God had reconsidered. It was never Abraham's intention to kill his son, and God never indicated whether he really wanted Abraham to kill Isaac, or whether he wanted Abraham to resist doing so. Given Abraham's moral purity and his assumption of God's justice and righteousness, we may reasonably conclude that if, at the very end, God had not rescinded his command for Isaac's death, Abraham would have rejected the command, chosen the moral course of not committing murder and saved his son—and then been forced to reexamine the prospects of his new religion, and the belief and faith on which it rested. Abraham was waiting for God to say, "Don't do it."

The text vividly shows Abraham playing for time. It does not compress the action from Abraham's receipt of God's command to his execution of it. The text does not simply say—as it easily could have— "The following morning Abraham took his son to Mount Moriah. But, as he was about to sacrifice his son ... " *Indeed, Abraham never agrees to accept this command and perform it.* Instead, the text describes Abraham going through a series of separate steps: First he gets up; then he dresses his animals; then he gets his retinue in order; then he cuts the firewood; and then he sets off; and then he sees Moriah; and then he instructs his retinue to wait; and then he takes the firewood and places it on Isaac's back; and then he takes "the fire and the knife"; and then he and Isaac walk (*vayelkhu*), *not* run, toward Moriah; and then there is a conversation between them; and then he makes the various preparations of the altar; and then he ties Isaac onto the altar; and then he stretches out his arm and then, finally, he raises the knife above his son. Does this plodding, detailed sequence of steps connote a man rushing off to do God's bidding? Hardly.

The point of the text is quite clear. At each step Abraham is waiting for God to evidence a change of mind, to withdraw his command.

When that is not forthcoming, Abraham takes the next step, and puts the Almighty to the next test—as it were—always showing obedience, always *giving God the opportunity* to make the moral statement that God does not want man to murder or commit other immoral acts in God's name. And, at the very end, when Abraham takes the last step before he would be forced by his conscience to stop and challenge God's command, the angelic order to stop finally comes.

This view is strongly supported in the Talmud, which portrays Abraham as praying to God on Mount Moriah that Isaac be saved— and, I believe, surely hoping and expecting that he would be.[6]

Those who argue that Abraham intended to kill Isaac before being stopped, cannot prove it from the *Akedah*, because Abraham never agreed to kill his son, and never had to. Had he done so and said, "I still believe in God," we would have had proof. We would also have had a religion to which few, perhaps none of us, could subscribe, because such a religion would never have endured.*

When God says, "Because you have done this thing, and have not withheld your son, your only son ... I will indeed bless you and ... multiply your progeny" (Genesis 22:16-17), he means that "You [Abraham] were willing to endure the confused agony of going ahead and acting in seeming obedience to my [God's] command, to the very point of killing Isaac—*with faith that I would never allow that to happen.*"** This is the same kind of faith that the children of Israel

---

*According to the midrash, Abraham's apparent obedience to God's command caused Sarah's death and Isaac's alienation from him forever after. Although Abraham and Isaac ascend Moriah together, the Torah emphasizes that Abraham "returned to his servants" alone (Genesis 22:19); Abraham and Isaac settle in different places and never speak to each other again.

**There are hints in the text that Abraham never intended to kill Isaac. For example, Abraham brings along two young men on the trip, presumably to guard Isaac and him— but why take along potential witnesses to a killing, and why the need for them on a trip at God's command? Going up Moriah, Abraham tells them: "*We* [Isaac and I] will ... return to you" (emphasis added). When Isaac asks Abraham, "Where is the lamb for the sacrifice?" Abraham answers, "God will find *for himself* the lamb," instead of "for us," suggesting that Isaac was in no danger if the lamb was not found, but *God* needed the lamb in order to retain his only follower, and the founder of the world religion that would spread God's message of ethical monotheism. Similarly, see Rashi on Genesis 12:1.

demonstrated when they plunged into the waters of the Red Sea at
God's command (Exodus 14:15-16)—not the serene faith that God
wanted them to kill themselves and their families by drowning, and
the zealous intention of doing so, but the confident faith that God
would, somehow, save them and keep his redemptive promises to
them. Such a faith demonstrates, as did Abraham's, that God is,
indeed, a God of justice and righteousness and not a God who tests
the faith of his followers by testing their willingness to kill themselves or their loved ones just because God asks it.

Abraham did not want God's moral law against murder to be affirmed
merely as a divine response to a human plea, as occurred at Sodom, or
to be proclaimed merely as a response to human arguments about God's
mercy, justice and righteousness. To achieve this, Abraham had to have
an enduring, unshakable faith in God's justice and righteousness, a faith
that allowed him to proceed with the *Akedah*, *not* with the steadfast,
zealous intent to kill Isaac,* but with the steadfast, confident faith that
God, *without the need for human pleading*, would ultimately pronounce for
all, and for all time, the prohibition against murder—even for God's
glory and in God's name.

The *Akedah* is a morality tale of Abraham's staunch defense of God's
moral law against any temptation—even God's command—to violate
it. It establishes Judaism's unique insight among ancient religions, cults

---

*Moreover, the Bible's use of angels, instead of God, to state that Abraham did not
"[intend to] withhold" his son, actually suggests the opposite conclusion. In Jewish tradition (based on the story of creation in Genesis and other biblical and talmudic sources),
angels—in contrast to man, who is born with free will—are perfect in their essence, and
therefore lack the capacity for or understanding of moral choice and intent. They can com-
prehend only human actions (see discussion of angels [*mal'akhim*] by Rabbi Chayyim
Hezekiah Medini [1833-1905], in his 18-vol. quasi-talmudic encyclopedia, *Sedei Chemed*).
Thus, for example, the angels objected to the creation of man because he is subject to sin,
and they cannot forgive a repentant sinner; they lack understanding of his temptation and
later change of heart (see Exodus 23:21 and the authoritative medieval biblical commentary of Rashi). The *Akedah*, therefore, is indirectly and subtly telling us that angels could
not have known what Abraham intended to do, and is contrasting their *mechanical obedience*
to God's will (evident by their believing and praising Abraham's apparent obedience to
God's command to kill Isaac) with Abraham's silent *moral response*—which was to question
and, if ultimately necessary, to resist that terrible command.

and cultures about the dangers of having human beings submit to the orders of individuals who claim unique access to the wishes of "the gods," or of any god.

The corrective is a religion based on a covenant between God and *all* of the people, in a revealed text to which *all* have access and which *all* can master. No person or elite can misguide the people down paths of immorality in the name of a supernatural power.

God was testing Abraham to see if he would remain faithful to God's revealed moral law even when divinely commanded to violate it, in order fully and finally to expunge the practice of child sacrifice or any murder (ostensibly) in God's name or for God's benefit. Abraham never intended to kill Isaac but, with faith in God's morality, Abraham was waiting for God to say, "Stop, don't do it, I didn't mean it," just as God was waiting for Abraham to say, "I won't do it."

In his determination not to kill Isaac, and his willingness to go forward with God's command until ordered to stop, Abraham demonstrated the strongest moral courage and the purest religious faith.

Reprinted from Bible Review, *October 1993.*

---

[1] Joseph B. Soloveitchik in *Man and Faith in the Modern World, Reflections of the Rav*, adapted from the lectures of Rabbi Joseph B. Soloveitchik by Abraham R. Besdin (Hoboken, NJ: Ktav, 1989), vol. 2, p. 50, quoting *Sifri* 313, *Ha'azinu.*

[2] Rashi, commentary on Genesis 24:7; Babylonian Talmud, *Berakhot* 59.

[3] Jerusalem Talmud, *Hagigah* 1:7; Gerson Cohen, *Studies in the Variety of Rabbinic Cultures* (Philadelphia: Jewish Publication Society, 1991), p. 73.

[4] Fania Fénelon with Marcelle Routier, *Playing for Time*, trans. Judith Landry (Berkley, NY: 1979).

[5] Compare the *aggadah* (homiletic interpretation) that Abraham rushed to kill his son, e.g., Rashi and J.H. Hertz, *The Pentateuch and Haftorahs* (London: Soncino, 1938), at Genesis 22:3, compounding the moral problem of the traditional interpretation.

[6] The Babylonian Talmud (*Ta'anit* 15a) records that on fast days called in response to community suffering, a drought for example, the Israelites prayed: "May He Who answered Abraham on Mount Moriah answer [us]," a prayer that is still recited as part of the Yom Kippur liturgy. The Jerusalem Talmud, as interpreted, similarly indicates that Abraham was praying for God to relieve him of the terrible command to kill his son (*Ta'anit* 2:4). While this tradition confirms that Abraham did not wish to kill Isaac, we must try to understand the text as it is written, in which Abraham remained silent about Isaac until the end of the *Akedah.*

3

ABRAHAM AND YAHWEH

A Case of Male Bonding

PHILIP R. DAVIES

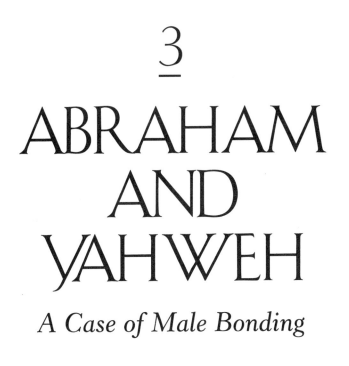

For centuries Abraham has been regarded as a paradigm of how a good Jew or Christian should behave—although moving house all the time (Genesis 12:4,10, 13:1,18, 20:1, et al.), pimping off your wife (Genesis 12:10-16) and agreeing to slaughter your child (Genesis 22) are not usually highlighted as examples to be followed. Could Abraham be a hero of the Christian Coalition? Alas, family values are not his strong point. But he does make a lot of money, and he has a private army. And he certainly believes in sacrifice—so long as it's an animal or someone else being sacrificed.

As this suggests, my reading of the story of Abraham is somewhat different from the conventionally pious reading. What we have in Genesis 11-25, I believe, is a story of male bonding, the story of a relationship between two males—Abraham and his God, Yahweh

(we'll call them Abraham* and Yahweh,** although they both change
their names during the story)—who, from beginning to end, try to
bluff each other.

Neither is entirely successful; each is too clever to be taken in by
the other, but they both keep trying anyway, because that is the way
males behave.

This kind of male bonding has become a cliché to anyone who
goes to the movies. Honesty and belief are feigned on both sides,
obedience and agreement are often overtly expressed, but in fact the
relationship is based on wary mistrust, reinforced by a certain respect
and cemented by a series of implicit bargains and compromises.

As we shall see, the story of Abraham is a delightful anatomy of
a certain kind of male twosome, two macho characters who come
together for their own purposes and go along with each other because
of mutual interest, a liking for each other's bluffing and a certain
sneaky regard for each other's deviousness. (If I were casting the
leads, I would go for Michael Douglas as Yahweh and Kurt Russell
as Abraham.)

Most readers of the Bible understand the story of Abraham to
start at the beginning of chapter 12 with the summons from Yahweh,
the so-called call of Abraham: "Now the Lord said to Abram, 'Go
from your country and your kindred and your father's house to the
land that I will show you'" (Genesis 12:1). But the story really begins
in chapter 11, which deals with the Tower of Babel as an explanation of why humans were scattered across the face of the earth.
Toward the end of chapter 11, we learn that Abraham was apparently born in Ur of a father named Terah. Ur is not explicitly identified here as Abraham's birthplace, but later (Genesis 15:7) Yahweh
says he called Abraham from Ur, so Abraham must have been born
there. (Actually, Yahweh didn't call him out of Ur, but let's pass on

*The patriarch's name is changed from Abram in Genesis 17:5.
**The deity is sometimes called Yahweh (usually translated as "the Lord") and sometimes
Elohim (translated as "God").

that for the moment.) By the time of the call (in chapter 12), Terah has already moved with his family to Haran. This move (described in chapter 11) is apparently part of Yahweh's strategy of scattering people across the face of the earth instead of concentrating them in lower Mesopotamia.[1] (See, also, Chapter 5, "Bible Versus Babel," by Jacob Milgrom.) But Yahweh's later statement that he called Abraham from Ur is really Yahweh 'fessing up that the move from Ur to Haran was part of his overall strategy. We are also told that when Terah left Ur with his family, he was heading for the land of Canaan. So the stop in Haran is a change of plan. This change is not Yahweh's doing, but Terah's.

At this point, with Terah and his family in Haran, Yahweh gives up on Terah; the *paterfamilias* is too old to move again. Terah named the city where he stopped Haran—after his dead son* (Genesis 11:28), Abraham's brother—so indicating that he is full of sentiment for his current abode. Yahweh simply decides to skip a generation (just as he will do with the "wilderness generation" [Numbers 14:26-31] and with Moses, leaving him on Mt. Nebo without taking him to the Promised Land [Numbers 27:13-15]; apparently this is a habit with this God): Instead of proceeding with Terah, Yahweh approaches Terah's sprightly 75-year-old son Abraham to attend to the unfinished business.

But Yahweh doesn't say, "It's time to finish off the journey you were supposed to make." He says instead, "Leave your country, relations and household, to go to somewhere I will show you" (Genesis 12:1). Yahweh doesn't even tell Abraham where he is supposed to go. Tantalizingly, he just calls it a place that "I will *show* you."

This directive is backed up with an inducement: Yahweh says, "If you do this, I'll make you, literally, a household name, and you will

---

*In Hebrew the names of the person and the city differ slightly, but the coincidence and the habit of naming lands and cities after persons (or vice versa) are well attested in the Hebrew Bible, so I suspect there is meant to be at least a wordplay here.

be the ancestor of a great nation" (Genesis 12:2). A promise is what theologians call this, but let's call it an inducement. It's a bit short on detail for a promise.

Saying nothing, Abraham simply gets up "to go to the land of Canaan" (Genesis 12:5). So Abraham *knows* what this unnamed land is and which way to walk. He doesn't ask the way because he knows perfectly well, but he doesn't let on to Yahweh that he knows. He goes along for his own reasons. Why, after all, live in your father's city, which is named after your elder brother, when you can have your own place and your own tribe named after you? Abraham appears simply to obey, but this is far from true. Don't forget, he takes with him not only his wife but also his nephew Lot (Haran's son). And he takes them despite having been told to leave his relatives behind (Genesis 12:1). (We worry about whether Sarah counts as a relative; this might depend on whether we really believe she was Abraham's sister, as he later claims.)

For Yahweh's part, so far he has only offered to *show* Abraham this land. Perhaps he intends to suggest more (will he *give* it to him?), perhaps not. In any event, Yahweh's offer turns out to be just the beginning of a protracted period of bargaining of the kind familiar to anyone who has tried to purchase a carpet in Jerusalem's Old City. Indeed, Yahweh's offer soon begins to look suspicious, for no sooner does Abraham reach Canaan than we learn that "the Canaanites are in the land" (Genesis 12:6). Well, you might say, who else *would* be in the land of Canaan but the Canaanites? Ah, but these distant lands were supposed to be unoccupied, as Haran was before Terah got there. These crafty Canaanites must have started, like everyone else, from the plain of Shinar after the Tower of Babel incident. But they must have overtaken Terah and his family when they holed up in Haran. If this is the land Abraham is supposed to live in, he seems to be too late.

After reaching Canaan and finding it already occupied, perhaps Abraham asks himself whether he should turn back. At least it is

24

logical to suppose that Yahweh thinks this is what Abraham might be thinking. Yahweh needs to say something quickly to keep Abraham on the hook, so Yahweh now undertakes not simply to "show" Abraham the land (Genesis 12:1) but to "give" the land to his descendants (Genesis 12:7). Not to Abraham, mind you, and *certainly* not to the Canaanites, but to Abraham's descendants! Pretty clever of Yahweh: He doesn't give the land to the people who happen to be around. Better not to involve anyone who is there at the time.

It's not difficult to imagine what Abraham must be wondering at this point: How and why did Yahweh let these Canaanites, my new neighbors, get the land? Did he promise it to *them* as well? Do they know it won't be theirs for long?

And another thing: Yahweh told Abraham at the time of the call that all the nations of the earth would be blessed through Abraham (Genesis 12:3). It no doubt occurred to Abraham, when he arrived in Canaan and found the Canaanites there, to ask himself: "How are *these* nations going to be blessed through me, as Yahweh said they would? By losing their land to my descendants? Surely that is not going to count."

Abraham's response to Yahweh's new offer is rather minimal. He doesn't say "Oh, Lord, you shouldn't! I don't deserve this! Just what I always wanted" or even "How much land *exactly* will my descendants get?" He doesn't even ask where all of this leaves *him*. What is *he* supposed to do while waiting for his descendants to be given this unspecified amount of land at an unspecified time and by unspecified means?

You would expect Abraham, if he thinks Yahweh is serious, simply to settle down where he is and begin to produce some descendants who will take over the place. But no. Instead, Abraham builds an altar, presumably offers a sacrifice and promptly moves on to Bethel, where he builds another altar, presumably makes another sacrifice and then moves further south (Genesis 12:7-9). Some animals mark their territory by dropping feces or urine; maybe patriarchs did it by building altars. But Abraham does not circumscribe a territory. Instead, he moves in a straight line to Egypt, out of the land he has just been promised, or nearly promised, in Genesis 12:10. Why? Because this promised land now has no food. Famines are, in the biblical worldview, caused by gods, so we must wonder why Yahweh brings a famine that forces his protégé out of the land. Maybe so Yahweh can reassure himself that he is in control of Abraham, *appearing* to dictate what the patriarch-to-be decides of his own accord to do anyway. (This is a ploy Yahweh resorts to several times with Abraham.) So Abraham enters Egypt.

But before crossing the border, he asks his wife (who we are told is very good-looking) to pose as his sister so he won't be killed (Genesis 12:11-13). Some commentators, anxious to defend everything Abraham does, suggest that he did not anticipate the outcome of this ruse. That is nonsense. Abraham's life is in danger, he says, because his wife is so desirable he might be killed for her. It follows that her masquerading as an *available* woman will inevitably lead to the consequences that do, in fact, ensue. Abraham can see perfectly well what is going to happen, and for the first time he openly instigates a chain of events entirely for his personal benefit. He shows no interest in either offspring or land. He has left the land and now disposes of his wife. It is known that she is barren (Genesis 11:30), but Abraham does nothing to find another woman on whom to beget offspring.

Soon enough we find out what Abraham *does* want, and it isn't anything he was promised. He wants to be rich. Business beats blessings any day.

Pharaoh takes Abraham's wife "into his house"—a nice euphemism—thinking that she is Abraham's sister, and Pharaoh treats Abraham quite nicely, thank you, "for her sake" (Genesis 12:15-16). As the patron of his "sister," Abraham receives the bride-price in return for her: "For her sake [Pharaoh] dealt well with Abraham," says the story, giving him herds of animals and servants.

Abraham likes this particular deception so much that he tries it again on another occasion (in chapter 20 he passes his wife off as his sister to Abimelech, king of Gerar—and it works again; Abraham gets sheep, oxen, servants and a thousand pieces of silver). He even passes the idea on to his son Isaac (who passes off his wife Rebekah as his sister to the same king [Genesis 26:7]).

Abraham is beginning to look like an unscrupulous entrepreneur, a get-rich-quick merchant, to whom descendants and long-term land possession are unimportant. No matter what Yahweh wants for him, *he*, Abraham, continues to pursue his own goals. The Egyptian episode shows that Abraham's and Yahweh's interests are not identical. This will be a key thread of the story: In effect, the rest of the story shows how each of them does his own thing, although they stick together for their mutual benefit.

Abraham, after all, seems happy with the arrangement. And maybe Sarah is too. Exchanging a wandering, selfish and uncaring husband for an appreciative and very rich sugar-pharaoh is not a bad deal. Pharaoh, too, seems happy with the new addition to his harem. He certainly pays Abraham plenty for it.

So who *isn't* happy? Well, Yahweh isn't. He believes *he* is writing the script, not Abraham. So he intervenes to restore his plot. Not, as pious readers suppose, to *save* anyone or anything. From what or whom is anyone to be saved? For Sarah's virtue it's too late, even if she wanted it to be saved. Abraham can only be saved from the terrible fate of getting richer every day without having to work. Yahweh can only save his own face. He wants Abraham to be in the land of Canaan thinking about descendants.

How can Yahweh get Abraham back there? He can't bribe or otherwise persuade Abraham to leave Egypt. And he can't fool him into it either. So he brings about Abraham's departure by other means. It's the old plague routine, which Yahweh seems to favor for changing the minds of pharaohs. Yahweh brings a plague on

Pharaoh and his house (Genesis 12:17). Pharaoh knows that Abraham is the cause, so he sends away Sarah, Abraham "and all that he [Abraham] had" (Genesis 12:17-20). Abraham and Sarah are thus banished from Egypt.

What's the score at this point? Yahweh wants Abraham in the land of Canaan, but Abraham wants to be rich. A compromise is reached—Abraham will be rich in Canaan: "Abram went up out of Egypt ... and Abram was very rich in cattle, in silver, and in gold" (Genesis 13:1-2). Our two males are now ready for the next round.

Another conflict arises almost immediately. Everything Abraham does suggests that he is very fond of his nephew Lot, from bringing him from Haran (contrary to divine instructions) to bringing him to Egypt and back. Abraham's general attitude makes the most sense if he believes Lot is his heir.[2] In any event, Abraham soon realizes that he and Lot have become so rich (Genesis 13:2,5) that the land is too small to support both of them (Genesis 13:6). And there is another factor to consider. The other inhabitants of the land are also growing: The place now has not only Canaanites but "Canaanites and Perizzites" (Genesis 13:7). Abraham proposes that he and Lot split the land, allowing Lot the choice of portion. Lot chooses the better half, which includes a place with wicked people —"great sinners against Yahweh" (Genesis 13:13). Wait a minute: Are these inhabitants supposed to know Yahweh? Their wickedness, however, is Yahweh's pretext for disliking Lot. There is a hint of Lot's exclusion from Yahweh's plans in the statement that "Abraham dwelt in the land of Canaan" (Genesis 13:12), which implies that Lot did not live there.

As long as Lot is around, Abraham does not worry about the promise of descendants. This obviously weakens Yahweh's bargaining position, so Yahweh must deprive Abraham of Lot. Accordingly, he undertakes a series of maneuvers intended to do just that. First, the land Lot chooses is blitzed (Genesis 14:11), and Lot himself is kidnapped (Genesis 14:12). When God destroys Sodom, Lot narrowly escapes with his life, but he loses his wife. (Well, he loses a wife and gains a pillar of salt, but that's not a great deal.) Lot ends up living in a cave with his two daughters, all he has left (Genesis 19:30). It is hard not to see Yahweh behind this chain of misfortunes. But Yahweh's aims are frustrated, foiled by members of Lot's family: Abraham rescues Lot, and Lot's daughters rescue his posterity.

Still, Yahweh makes it clear to Abraham that he will give *him* and *his* descendants the land as far as he can see (Genesis 13:15). Not Lot or his descendants. This is actually the first time Abraham himself has been promised the land. The attentive reader will observe that each divine promise differs from the previous one: If you're a deity, you are only as good as your last promise. But that hardly explains why virtually every chapter opens with another promise or a new version of the previous one. Yahweh must be a compulsive promise maker, a neurotic covenant maker. Making offers, finding out what motivates people, is part of his personality. In fact, that is actually his main tactic for controlling humans. Some people (ancient and modern) are fooled into believing he has kept his promises, despite all the evidence to the contrary.

But this constant promising has little effect on Abraham. Abraham was not born yesterday. He is told to wander through the length and breadth of the land now promised to him personally. So how does he react? Not unreasonably, he is unimpressed. The non-Abrahamic population is growing, and since Lot's departure Abraham has no descendants living in the land. In any case, he has been promised land only "as far as he can see" (Genesis 13:15). This is not really very much land for a man with immense flocks and herds and silver. You can't actually see all that far from Bethel. And so, when Yahweh invites him to take a tour of the most recently promised territory (Genesis 13:17), he declines and moves instead from Bethel to Hebron, some 30 miles south, which you certainly can't see from Bethel (Genesis 13:18). He builds an altar there (of course) and decides to stay put. We observe again that Abraham is a man following his own agenda, and all of his sacrifices cannot disguise his basic disregard for Yahweh's plans.

Yahweh must realize by this time what a difficult partner he has in Abraham. Abraham has foiled Yahweh's ploy to remove Lot and ended up with even greater wealth. Abraham not only rescued Lot from the aggressors, but also brought back all the loot that they had taken from Sodom and Gomorrah. Indeed, this is mentioned before Lot is brought back: Abraham "brought back all the goods, and *also* brought back his kinsman Lot" (Genesis 14:16). Abraham gives his ally Melchizedek, the king of Salem, a tenth of the booty—presumably both goods and people. The king of Sodom, apparently offered the remainder, offers to take the people and leave the goods to Abraham, but the patriarch does not need the spoils of his allies; he takes only what his own men acquired. Here is a seriously rich man who does not need the small change offered to him by the king of Sodom. Abraham's generosity is the generosity of the extremely affluent. And he made it himself—he's a self-made rich man.

Somehow, Yahweh needs to reassert divine control over the triumphant Abraham. And so, after Abraham has easily defeated four foreign kings with his own private A-Team (Genesis 14) and made it clear how filthy rich he is, Yahweh comes with the promise, "Don't be afraid, Abraham, I'm your shield and you will have a big reward" (Genesis 15:1). A bit tame, isn't it?

For the first time, Abraham actually bothers to answer back. He asserts the obvious—that he doesn't have a son (Genesis 15:2). This comment, though, is not a disguised plea: Abraham is in the driver's seat at this point, so he can afford a rebuke, to the effect of "Let's cut the crap; you and I know that these promises of yours are not really serious, they're just part of the game." He even adds to the insult by telling Yahweh he has already decided who his heir will be—one of his own servants, Eliezer, the steward of his house (Genesis 15:2).

Up to this point, there has been no overt confrontation, no defiance. But this provocative response, this outburst of temper, is unwise because it will destroy the relationship unless it is immediately resolved. Gods can't allow humans to say publicly that they don't take them seriously. In the thought-world of the Bible, gods need humans, but humans need gods, too. So both sides must cool it, or the plot can't move on and there will be no Israel and no Bible and no Judeo-Christian culture.

Yahweh makes the first move by saying that Abraham will have a son and that his seed will be as numerous as the stars (Genesis 15:4-5). Abraham needs to make a gesture too—and he does just that: "Abraham believed this, and it was reckoned to him as righteousness" (Genesis 15:6). (In the movie version of the story, Abraham would probably say something like, "OK, I believe you. I'm sorry," and Yahweh would say, "Fine, forget it, you're a decent guy." The two males would then embrace.)

But it doesn't quite work out as neatly as that because Yahweh goes over the top: He tells Abraham that he called him from Ur to *give* him the land (Genesis 15:7). Abraham is a bit offended: Yahweh hadn't said anything of the kind in Haran (although, as we saw, Abraham knew the score). Yahweh had said only that he would *show* him the land (Genesis 12:1). Abraham remembers quite well what was said and that he was not originally promised the land. So Abraham is again reminded that he is dealing with a duplicitous deity who lied to him then and is lying to him now about the past. Having "believed" in Yahweh for about one verse (Genesis 15:6), Abraham now remembers whom he is dealing with and demands a bit of proof. "How am I to know that I will occupy it?" he asks (Genesis 15:8). This is not "believing": This is asking for proof, exactly the opposite!

The struggle for the upper hand is still on. Will Abraham get his proof? Certainly not! Yahweh cannot afford to lose face as well as credibility. So he reasserts his superiority by demonstrating his divine rank, impressing Abraham with a few special effects: Birds of prey come down, and Abraham scares them off; at sunset he falls asleep, and a great darkness descends upon him; then Abraham hears that, after all, the promises of the land will come *not* to his immediate descendants but to the fourth generation, after some unpleasant adventures (Genesis 15:11-13). After a few more effects—a smoking pan and a flaming torch—Abraham hears that his descendants will be given a huge amount of land, from the Euphrates to the Egyptian border (Genesis 15:18).

This seems like the right kind of psychological pressure: Scare him a bit, put off the promise, tell him everything will be more difficult, then finally make the prize a bit bigger. But in spelling this out, Yahweh lets slip that the original single Canaanite nation (which later became two—Canaanites and Perizzites) has now become ten (Genesis 15:19-21)! Their iniquities may be piling up, but their immigration rate is too. This may be part of Yahweh's plan, of course. He is a deity, after all; he has a lot of other things on his plate. He has other people to deal with besides Abraham.

But what Yahweh has really done, from Abraham's point of view, is to confirm that even solemn and oft-repeated divine promises won't necessarily be kept. There are conditions, involving other deals with other nations and specified but undisclosed amounts of iniquity. It seems that this is the reward for daring to ask a deity for proof.

We, the readers, *know*, as Abraham only suspects, that even these promises are false: The promised extent of the land is never given to his descendants. Indeed, no land at all is occupied within the promised time frame.

"How shall I know?" Abraham had asked. But he got only vultures, darkness and a slightly more detailed promise. Nevertheless, the relationship has been restored rather than destroyed. The underlying negotiating positions are clear once again: Yahweh says, "Trust me," and Abraham says nothing (but possibly smiles). Each partner knows the other is holding something back. What keeps them

passing off Sarah as his sister again. And Yahweh struck back. But now it's time for a real lesson; Yahweh wants to force Abraham to admit that he cares for his son Isaac and for Yahweh's promises of offspring. He wants Abraham to plead, or even to disobey, so that he can forgive him, play the deity and finally assert the authority of the divine over the human.

But Yahweh loses this bout because Abraham has a trump card: Isaac is more important to Yahweh than he is to Abraham. We realize this when Yahweh sends Abraham to "one of the hills I will tell you" (Genesis 22:2), echoing Yahweh's call to Abraham to go to a land that he would be shown (Genesis 12:1). There Abraham is to sacrifice Isaac, "the son whom you love" (Genesis 22:2). Note that it is Yahweh who asserts Abraham's love for Isaac, not Abraham. Abraham, once again, merely complies—without a word of protest. But, as when he was initially called, Abraham's behavior does not indicate blind obedience. Although we have been given no reason to think that Abraham is particularly fond of Isaac, Yahweh does not think for a minute that Abraham will obey this crazy command. He expects Abraham to protest his love for Isaac and ask to be let off. Look how Abraham bargained for Sodom and Gomorrah. Abraham, for his part, knows Yahweh will not let Isaac die. After all, whose idea was Isaac anyway, if not Yahweh's? Yahweh wouldn't even let Ishmael die in the womb; he ordered the pregnant Hagar to return to Abraham's house after Sarah had treated her harshly and she had fled.

So Abraham forces Yahweh to the brink and makes *him* intervene. When Isaac asks, "Where is the lamb for a burnt offering?" Abraham replies, "God will provide for himself the lamb for the offering, my son" (Genesis 22:7-8; plate 2, p. 79). There is no irony here—or, rather, there is a double irony. Abraham says what he knows to be true: Yahweh will not let it happen. Perhaps, too, he knows Yahweh is listening, and he is teasing Yahweh. That would add to the fun and to the score.

Everyone knows that Yahweh relents in the end, although most people don't appreciate that Abraham faces him down. Yahweh stays Abraham's hand as he raises the knife (Genesis 22:10-12; plates 1 and 3, pp. 79 and 80). Later Jewish embellishment of this story was quite right to redirect the focus of attention to Isaac. He alone *did* behave well. Just like Abimelech, Isaac, the one decent person in the game, suffers as the result of two males playing poker with each other.

So Yahweh backs down; Abraham has successfully called his bluff and won the contest. What can Yahweh do now? Deities aren't supposed to lose. He can only save face by playing his favorite card: "Because you have done this, you will indeed have what I promised anyway" (Genesis 22:15-19). Pretending that this was a test Abraham had to pass in order for the promise to be fulfilled, and that what was already promised is now a reward, is about the best Yahweh can do to relieve the situation. True, Yahweh has managed to persuade theological commentators that he really won, but victory over such a weak audience is no compensation for defeat by a real man like Abraham, who emerges from my reading looking much better than from the usual one: Abraham knew that he wouldn't have to kill Isaac and that Yahweh was only bluffing.

The story is nearly over. The storyteller can't help telling us how many children Abraham's brother had (Genesis 22:20-24). What good is it to Abraham to know that while his *one* son is *not* being sacrificed after all, Nahor is busy siring *eight* sons? The very next event, in chapter 23, is the death of Sarah and her burial in her own special cave. Maybe prompted by her death, Abraham at last begins to take care of his second son: We have a long account of the search for a wife for Isaac.

Then Abraham proceeds to sire six more sons by another wife, Keturah (Genesis 25:1-2). But he sends all of them away and bequeaths everything to Isaac. Is this a final gesture of submission, acceding to the divine wish that only Isaac is to inherit? Has the old schemer at last given in? He is, after all, very old, very blessed, very rich and perhaps very tired. The only thing left for him is to die.

I hate to think of the story ending this way, mostly because of my sympathy for this Abraham character. But on reflection, it does seem right that at the end of his life, Abraham voluntarily does what Yahweh wants. He has no more points to make. He realizes, perhaps, that he has no land except the land he bought with his own money and that he is not going to get any more land, promises or no. But then, he had never taken these promises for anything more than what they were, cards in a game. As in all good male-bonding stories, the partners grow old (unless one of them is a deity) and make peace. The children will have to negotiate with this same deity, and the father hopes they will have as much success as he; there is no need to stack the deck against them. It's a satisfying ending—the human voluntarily quits while he is ahead, when there is nothing more to be won. He realizes that although he will die, his deity will not.

I find this story of male bonding convincing, clever and entertaining. But can I draw a serious moral from it, a moral comparable to the great moral "truths" found by the writers of numerous commentaries and tracts?

Why should I? A story doesn't have to have a moral. But here is one, anyway. It's a moral for people who think Yahweh might be real rather than a character in some ancient writings and who reckon they, too, have to deal with him: Learn from this story; learn from your predecessor. Don't trust this God. He doesn't trust you and won't tell you the truth. He is in the business of making promises that are never fulfilled. Abraham did not achieve the ambition imposed on him—to populate the world and receive his own allotment of land. But he *knew* that; he recognized that the promises were a kind of running gag, no more. Deities, like politicians, try to keep us dangling in the hope of things to come, with promises renewed, altered, repeated, revoked, supplied with new conditions.

Be wise, like Abraham. Take everything this (or any) deity says with a pillar of salt. Your weak card is your belief and trust in him. If you really believe in what he says, you will lose. But if you call his bluff, pretend to go along with him while keeping your own counsel and taking whatever he decides to give you, you will prosper. If he wants to bless you, do not object; but let it not deter you from your own course or seduce you into groveling gratitude. Don't be like some of Abraham's descendants, physical and spiritual, who still believe in Abraham's God and who still look forward to his promises being fulfilled. One of them is born every minute.

Reprinted from Bible Review, *August 1995.*

[1]The connection between the Babel and Abraham stories has been made by Thomas L. Thompson, in *The Origin Tradition of Ancient Israel* (Sheffield: JSOT Press, 1987), pp. 79-80.

[2]As argued by David J.A. Clines, in "The Ancestress in Danger," in *What Does Eve Do to Help? and Other Readerly Questions to the Old Testament* (Sheffield: JSOT Press, 1990), pp. 61-84, esp. 71-73.

4

ABRAHAM'S EIGHT CRISES

*The Bumpy Road to Fulfilling
God's Promise of an Heir*

LARRY R. HELYER

he Abraham cycle (Genesis 11:27-25:11) is a drama of
increasing tension—a tension between Yahweh's promise
that Abraham would have an heir, indeed, that he would
become the father of many nations, and the threat to the
fulfillment of that promise by a series of crises. The literary technique employed is what Peter Ellis calls "the obstacle story":

> Few literary techniques have enjoyed so universal and perennial a
> vogue as the obstacle story. It is found in ancient and modern litera-
> ture from the Gilgamesh epic and the *Odyssey* to the *Perils of Pauline*
> and the latest novel. Its character is episodal. [The episodes are] not
> self-contained but find [their] *raison d'être* in relation to the larger
> story or narrative of which [they are] a part. [The] purpose is to
> arouse suspense and sustain interest by recounting episodes which
> threaten or retard the fulfillment of what the reader either suspects or
> hopes or knows to be the ending of the story.[1]

What ties the entire Abraham cycle together is the problem of an heir. Yahweh's promise of posterity to Abram (Genesis 12:2) highlights the question: Who will be Abram's heir?

Although this problem runs through the entire cycle as a leit-motif, it is not the only issue. A subtheme relates to the promise of the land of Canaan. Throughout the cycle, we are reminded of the delay: "At that time the Canaanites and the Perizzites lived in the land" (Genesis 13:7; cf. 12:6, 15:19,20). Yahweh's command to "walk through the length and breadth of the land, for I will give it to you" (Genesis 13:17; cf. 12:6) underscores the fact that the only portion of land Abram owned outright was a burial plot at Machpelah, which he bought to bury his wife Sarah (Genesis 23:17-20). His life as a pastoral semi-nomad poignantly emphasizes the great gulf between promise and fulfillment. When, however, we inquire as to the leading theme of the Abraham cycle, we have no hesitation: It is the problem of an heir.

Even before Abram's call in Genesis 12:1, we are told that "Sarai [as she was then named] was barren; she had no child" (Genesis 11:30). Following hard on the heels of this problem comes God's promise, "I will make of you a great nation" (Genesis 12:2). Thus the tension between the promise of God and the problem of Abram.

The author skillfully and artistically maintains this tension throughout the entire cycle by a series of eight crises. Each crisis threatens to revoke the promise. Abraham and Sarah live out their lives in this narrative world of despair and hope. Occasionally, they illustrate the folly of human initiatives, but ultimately they tri-umphantly testify to the faithfulness of Yahweh in keeping his covenant promise. Still, by the time the cycle has run its course, the fulfillment of the promise is only partial: Isaac must carry on the promise, Jacob must survive his brother's murderous designs, Jacob's sons must survive a famine in Canaan followed by bondage in Egypt, and so on. In a sense, all of the Hebrew Scriptures carry forward this tension between promise and fulfillment.

The first crisis is occasioned by a drought in the Promised Land shortly after Abraham and Lot arrive there. Israel, like southern California, has a two-season climate: a rainy season, running from October to April; and a hot, dry season, running from June through August (September and May are transitional months). Most of the rain falls between December and February. The success of the farmer and herder, however, depends on the critical "early rain" (October-November) and the "later rain" (March-April) (see Deuteronomy 11:14). The former softens the ground, allowing the farmer to plow and plant his seed. The latter gives the emerging crops a needed boost before the long, rainless summer sets in. Failure at either end spells disaster. Shortly after Abram and Lot arrive in Canaan, they experience what must have been an especially severe drought. Little or no grass is available for their sizable flocks and herds. To save their livestock, they must head for the Nile River delta. This Abram does, but not without some misgivings.

Abram fears that the Egyptians will murder him for his beautiful wife Sarai, so he passes her off as his sister.[2] Pharaoh, captivated by Sarai's beauty, takes her into his harem. For his part, Abram is treated as a highly regarded tribal chieftain and he becomes the recipient of Pharaoh's largesse (Genesis 12:16). Only divine intervention reunites Abram with his wife. Abram, however, must own up to his duplicity before Pharaoh and suffer the indignity of being unceremoniously deported from the country (Genesis 12:19-20). (Abram's brief sojourn in Egypt is a preview of coming attractions. There will be another, longer stay by the Hebrews in Egypt, where they will be enslaved, but again they will leave with a considerable amount of Egyptian wealth [Exodus 12:25-36].)*

The story of Abraham's relationship to his nephew Lot should be understood in the context of the problem of an heir. Lot has been with his uncle Abram since they lived together in Ur of the Chaldees

---

*The Egyptians reclaimed a great amount of Israelite treasure when Pharaoh Shishak invaded the Land of Israel several hundred years later (see 1 Kings 14:25-26).

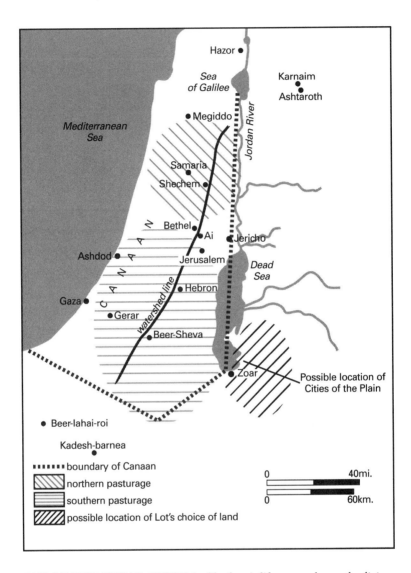

Hazor •

Sea
of Galilee

Karnaim
•
Ashtaroth

Jordan River

Mediterranean
Sea

• Megiddo

Samaria

Shechem •

C A N A A N

Bethel •
• Ai

• Jericho

Ashdod •

Jerusalem
•

Dead
Sea

watershed line

• Hebron

Gaza •

• Gerar

• Beer-Sheva

• Zoar

Possible location of
Cities of the Plain

• Beer-lahai-roi

Kadesh-barnea
•

▪▪▪▪▪▪ boundary of Canaan

northern pasturage

southern pasturage

possible location of Lot's choice of land

0   40mi.

0   60km.

ONE OF THE GREAT CRISES in Abraham's life occurred over the divi-
sion of the land (Genesis 13:5-11). When Lot, Abraham's nephew, is given
first choice, he selects neither the northern pasturage area nor the southern pas-
tures, but the well-watered plain of the Jordan River (the Cities of the Plain)—
outside of the Promised Land altogether. This crisis, explains author Larry
Helyer, is not really about land; it is about Abraham's inheritance. When Lot
moves out of the Promised Land, Abraham is left without an apparent heir.

44

(Genesis 11:31). The episode in Genesis 13 involving Lot's separation from Abram is indeed the second crisis. Abram's and Lot's flocks and herds have grown to such an extent that the land can no longer support both of them; moreover, there is strife between the herders of the two men (Genesis 13:6-7). To settle the matter, Abram proposes that the "land" be divided (Genesis 13:8-9). He gives his nephew first choice: Lot chooses the well-watered plain of the Jordan River (Genesis 13:10-11).

One common interpretation of the story is that Lot simply chooses the most desirable portion of the Promised Land. In this reading, then, Lot is an ungrateful opportunist, forcing his uncle to live the rugged life of a semi-nomad rather than the more sedate life of a city dweller, the life Lot picks, in the oasis of the Jordan Valley—a kind of Near East Palm Springs!

Other commentators argue that the real point of the story is that the promise of the land of Canaan to Abram and his offspring hangs in the balance, owing to Abram's magnanimous gesture in allowing Lot to have the first choice. In this interpretation, the land that Lot chooses is not in Canaan. Had Lot chosen the land of Canaan, so this interpretation goes, Abram would have been exiled to the plain of the Jordan. Providentially, Lot does not select the land of Canaan, and thus God's promise to Abram is secured.

Neither of these interpretations focuses on the real issue at stake—the problem of an heir. That is the context in which this episode must be understood. I agree with the second interpretation—that the land Lot chooses is not a part of the Promised Land. But this choice must be understood in the context of the overarching narrative framework.

To appreciate the implication of Lot's choice, we must understand a little of what scholars call historical geography. As the Genesis narratives indicate, the land of Canaan included two primary regions west of the Jordan River where the patriarchs grazed their flocks—one in the north and one in the south (see map, opposite page).

The northern area centered on Shechem (Genesis 12:6, 33:18-34:31, 37:12-17), with the Bethel-Ai region as the southern boundary. The southern area included Hebron/Mamre and the still more southerly region around Beer-Sheva and Gerar (Genesis 12:9, 13:1,18, 20:1, etc.). The two areas were effectively connected by the watershed line, the mountainous spine that runs through central Canaan. Movement between the two major pasturages followed this time-honored ridge route.

Abram and Lot make their agreement between Bethel and Ai, in the heart of Canaan. Abram offers Lot either the northern area or the southern area. Abram permits Lot to choose the portion of "the whole land" (kol-ha'areṣ) that he desires; for Abram, "the whole land" is the land of Canaan ('eres-kᵉna'an) (Genesis 13:9,12). To Abram's surprise—and dismay—Lot chooses neither! Lot chooses a third area—not in the land of Canaan (Genesis 13:10-11). This is clearly implied in the statement that "Abram settled in the land of Canaan, while Lot settled among the Cities of the Plain and moved his tent as far as Sodom" (Genesis 13:12).

Moreover, the biblical text is clear that the eastern boundary of Canaan is the Jordan River from its exit at the Sea of Galilee (the Kinnereth) to the Dead Sea (Salt Sea); from the southeastern end of the Dead Sea the border ran in a southwesterly direction toward Kadesh Barnea and then turned toward the Mediterranean, running along the Brook (or Wadi) of Egypt (cf. Numbers 34:1-29; Joshua 15:1-14; Ezekiel 47:13-20). In Genesis 14, as we shall see, Abram and Lot are involved in a war fought against the Cities of the Plain, which form a discrete political unit apart from the cities of Canaan.

The actual location of the notorious Cities of the Plain has been much debated. Until recently, most scholars assumed that, if any such cities ever existed, they must have been located beneath the waters of the southern end of the Dead Sea.[3] Now, however, Walter Rast and Thomas Schaub have cautiously advanced a new location:[4] They suggest five sites on the eastern side of the Ghor (the plain south of the Dead Sea).* Each site displays a thick destruction layer dated to either the end of Early Bronze III or the beginning of Early Bronze IV (c. 2350 B.C.E.). Whether or not these are the Cities of the Plain referred to in the Bible, the biblical tradition clearly indicates that they formed a distinct geopolitical entity, separate from the land of Canaan.

With this geographical background, we may better appreciate the import of the episode: Lot chooses a portion outside the Promised Land.

But there is more to it than this: Until this time, Uncle Abram had acted as a surrogate father to Lot. Lot's father, Haran, had died in Ur (Genesis 11:28). Lot went with Abram from Ur to Haran and then to the land of Canaan (Genesis 11:31, 12:4). Throughout chapters 12 and 13, the relationship between Abram and Lot is a close one. The text easily allows us to infer Abram's sense of responsibility for his nephew. Remember that Abram was otherwise childless. Mesopotamian law codes allowed for the adoption of an heir in the case of childlessness.[5] In all probability Abram regarded Lot as his heir.[6]

Abram's first solution to the problem of an heir, therefore, was to take Lot as his heir. Let's call this Plan A. When Abram's heir-apparent virtually eliminates himself from the promise by leaving the land of Canaan, Abram is without an heir. Plan A is scrapped. Yet, just at this juncture ("after Lot had separated from him" [Genesis 13:14]), Yahweh reaffirms the promise of the land to *Abram's offspring* ("your offspring" [Genesis 13:15]).

The third crisis finds Abram entangled in a Middle Eastern war. Genesis 14 describes the war near the Dead Sea between an alliance of the kings of the five Cities of the Plain and an alliance of Mesopotamian kings. In the course of battle, Lot is captured and

*The sites are Bab edh-Dhra, es-Safi (Zoar), Numeira, Feifa(eh) and Khanazir, all Early Bronze Age (3150-2200 B.C.E.) sites overlooking a wadi that drains into the Dead Sea.

taken prisoner. When Abram, now at Mamre, hears of this, he takes 318 retainers with him to rescue Lot. Although the rescue effort succeeds, Abram exposes himself to the endemic plague of the region—revenge and retaliation.[7] Fear of retaliation provides the backdrop for the divine oracle of Genesis 15:1: "Do not be afraid, Abram. I am your shield; your reward shall be very great." Yahweh will not abandon his covenant partner, and the Mesopotamian coalition never returns to settle the score. The third crisis is over.

But Abraham still does not have an heir, as he immediately reminds God: "O Lord God, what will you give me, for I continue childless?" (Genesis 15:2). Apparently Abram resorts to another human initiative—the adoption of one of his household slaves, Eliezer, as his heir: "The heir of my house is Eliezer of Damascus ... A slave born in my house is to be my heir," he says (Genesis 15:2-3). We might call this Plan B. To Abram's surprise, however, this initiative, too, is set aside with God's startling announcement: "This man shall not be your heir; no one but your own issue shall be your heir" (Genesis 15:4). The Lord then expands the promise to include innumerable descendants and confirms it in a symbolic covenant-ratification ceremony (Genesis 15:7-21). In one of the great moments in biblical history, Yahweh pledges himself unconditionally to fulfill the covenant promise: "To your descendants I give this land" (Genesis 15:18).

But of course Abram still has no descendants. Like a chime, the narrator immediately reminds us of the great problem of faith: "Now Sarai, Abram's wife, bore him no children" (Genesis 16:1). Another human initiative, this time sponsored by Sarai, sets the stage for the fourth crisis. Sarai will provide an heir not through her own body, but through her handmaid Hagar (Genesis 16:2). Sarai resorts to the legally accepted procedure of concubinage to assure a male heir.[8] This we might call Plan C—Sarai's contribution to the nagging problem of childlessness.

But just when things begin to look promising, and Hagar becomes pregnant, a conflict develops between the secondary wife and her mistress. Hagar may well have harbored notions of replacing Sarai as the primary wife. Sarai is given the authority to discipline the upstart Hagar severely.[9] Although pregnant, Hagar flees into the unforgiving desert south of Beer-Sheva. The survival of Hagar—and her unborn child—is at stake. Will the potential heir perish? Again the Lord intervenes. An angel of the Lord tells Hagar to "return to your mistress and submit to her" (Genesis 16:9); the angel promises Hagar that her descendants shall be a multitude. Hagar returns and bears Ishmael.

After this episode, Yahweh reaffirms his promise to Abram, the fifth such affirmation (Genesis 17:1-8). Abram's name is changed to Abraham (apparently the narrator understands "Abraham" to mean "ancestor of a multitude"; the new name reflects the covenant promise). In addition, a new element is instituted as a sign of the covenant relationship—Abraham is circumcised and the commandment of circumcision is imposed on all his offspring throughout the generations as a sign of the covenant (Genesis 17:9-27).

At this point, Ishmael appears to be Abraham's heir. Indeed, Abraham seems ready to accept this: "Abraham said to God, 'O that Ishmael might live in your sight!'" (Genesis 17:18). Then follows the astonishing promise that *Sarah* (whose name has been changed from Sarai) will bear Abraham's heir: "God said, 'No, but your wife Sarah shall bear you a son, and you shall name him Isaac'" (Genesis 17:19). Ishmael is rejected as the heir to the covenant promise. Plan C is effectively shelved.

Chapters 18 and 19 provide an interlude in the development of the story line. Among other things, they prolong the suspense. Chapter 18 describes the visit of the angels who prophesy that Sarah will give birth to a son even though she is now about 90 years old (Genesis 17:17). God also confides in Abraham about his plan to destroy Sodom and Gomorrah; Abraham bargains with God to save the cities, but not even ten righteous men can be found there. In chapter 19, the angels visit Lot in Sodom and provide for his escape before the city is destroyed. Lot's incestuous relationship with his daughters results in the birth of the ancestors of Israel's hated enemies, the Ammonites and the Moabites.

For our purposes, however, the important point is the announcement that Sarah will give birth to a son, despite her advanced age and the fact that "it had ceased to be with Sarah after the manner of women" (Genesis 18:11). A rhetorical question accompanies the announcement: "Is anything too difficult for the Lord?" (Genesis 18:14a).

Chapter 20 plunges us into the fifth crisis. Shortly after the announcement of the birth-to-be, Sarah winds up in another man's harem! Abraham has again passed off his wife as his sister—this time to Abimelech, the king of Gerar. Readers may be forgiven for wondering how Abimelech could find the 90-year-old Sarah so attractive. It seems too cynical to say it was purely a political marriage and too incredible to suggest something like Oil of Olay—some things are best left unexplained! The storyline leads us to assume, however, that if a son is born, he will be reckoned as Abimelech's heir, not Abraham's. Yahweh intervenes yet another time, however. He comes to Abimelech in a dream and tells him that Sarah is really Abraham's wife. Through God's intervention (perhaps through some sexual dysfunction), Abimelech was prevented from having intercourse with Sarah ("It was I who kept you from sinning," God tells Abimelech in a dream). Sarah is returned to Abraham, and the text tells us, "God healed Abimelech, and also healed his wife and female slaves so that they bore children" (Genesis 20:6,17).

As chapter 21 opens, the tension that has been sustained for so long eases: "The Lord dealt with Sarah as he had said, and the Lord did for Sarah as he had promised. Sarah conceived and bore Abraham a son in his old age" (Genesis 21:1-2). All is not well, however. Before long, the status of Ishmael vis-à-vis Isaac becomes a divisive issue in Abraham's household and provokes the sixth crisis. Though it grieves Abraham, at Sarah's insistence he disinherits and dismisses Ishmael. Apparently, Abraham grants Hagar and her son their freedom as compensation. This clears the field: There are no potential rivals to Isaac as Abraham's sole heir.

The seventh crisis comes as a shock. It comes when least expected. And it is unthinkable. After all obstacles have been overcome and all potential rivals eliminated, God demands Abraham's only son as a burnt offering. For Abraham, this is the moment of truth. Can he trust God to fulfill his promise despite this command, which seems to negate everything God stands for? We plod with Abraham up the slopes of Mt. Moriah, step by tortured step. The drama reaches its climax in the uplifted knife of Abraham. Suddenly God speaks: "Because you have done this, and have not withheld your son, your only son, I will indeed bless you, and I will make your offspring as numerous as the stars of heaven and the sand ... on the seashore" (Genesis 22:16-17).

God's intervention and the reaffirmation of his promise would seem to conclude the Abraham cycle at the moment when faith triumphs over all obstacles. In what may appear to be an anticlimactic episode, however, the narrative continues. Abraham's beloved wife Sarah dies. The promise of the land, we are reminded, has not been fulfilled. Abraham must purchase some land in which to bury her: "I am a stranger," he says, "an alien residing among you; give me property among you for a burying place" (Genesis 23:4). Abraham purchases Machpelah for 400 silver shekels. This is the only part of Canaan for which he can produce a deed!

The eighth and final crisis concerns finding a bride for Isaac (Genesis 24). Isaac must "not get a wife ... from the daughters of the Canaanites," says Abraham (Genesis 24:3). He decides to send his trusted servant (is this Eliezer?) back to Mesopotamia to get a wife for Isaac among Abraham's kindred. The problem is expressed by the servant: What if she won't come to Canaan? Should I bring Isaac back to the land from which you came? he asks Abraham (Genesis 24:5). The answer is an emphatic no. Isaac must stay in the land of promise and must not marry a Canaanite woman. Happily, when Rebekah is asked whether she will come to Canaan to be Isaac's wife, she agrees (plate 4, p. 80). The Abraham cycle ends with the statement that "Abraham gave all that he had to Isaac" (Genesis 25:5). The heir assumes his inheritance.

Long ago, the story began with Sarai's barrenness: "Now Sarai was barren; she had no child" (Genesis 11:30). It concludes: "After the death of Abraham, God blessed his son Isaac" (Genesis 25:11). The Abraham cycle underscores Yahweh's faithfulness to his covenant promise. It demonstrates that Israel exists only because of divine intervention. Divine initiative, however, calls for a response—a response of faith and commitment. Abraham is supremely a man of faith.

Reprinted from Bible Review, *October 1995.*

[1]Peter Ellis, *The Yahwist, the Bible's First Theologian* (Notre Dame: Fides, 1968), p. 136.

[2]Ephraim A. Speiser's interpretation of the sistership documents of Nuzi and their relationship to Genesis is defended in his commentary, *Genesis*, The Anchor Bible Series (Garden City, NY: Doubleday, 1964), pp. 91-92. This view is now rejected by most scholars. See Cecil J. Mullo Weir, "The Alleged Hurrian Wife-Sister Motif in Genesis," *Transactions of the Glasgow University Oriental Society* 22 (1967), pp. 14-25.

[3]See James P. Harland, "Sodom and Gomorrah: The Location and Destruction of the Cities of the Plain," *Biblical Archaeologist* (*BA*) 5 (1942), pp. 17-32, and *BA* 6 (1943), pp. 41-54.

[4]Walter E. Rast and R. Thomas Schaub, *Survey of the Southeastern Plain of the Dead Sea, 1973, Annual of the Department of Antiquities of Jordan* 19 (1974). See Willem C. van Hattem, "Once Again: Sodom and Gomorrah," *BA* 44 (1981), pp. 87-92; Rast and Schaub, "On the New Site Identifications for Sodom and Gomorrah," *Biblical Archaeology Review*, Jan./Feb. 1981, p. 18.

[5]See James B. Pritchard, ed., *Ancient Near Eastern Texts Relating to the Old Testament*, 3rd ed. with supplement (Princeton, NJ: Princeton Univ. Press, 1969) (*ANET*), p. 220, for an example of adoption at Nuzi, and p. 174 (sections 185-193) for adoption documents in Hammurabi's law code. See also Sabatino Moscati, *Ancient Semitic Civilizations* (New York: G.P. Putnam's Sons, 1957), p. 83, and Ephraim A. Speiser, *Annual of the American Schools of Oriental Research* 10 (1930), pp. 7-13. For an example of a man at Ugarit who adopted his grandson, see Isaac Mendelsohn, "A Ugaritic Parallel to the Adoption of Ephraim and Manasseh," *Israel Exploration Journal* 9 (1959), pp. 180-183.

[6]A point made by Rashi in his commentary on the Pentateuch and cited in *The Soncino Chumash* (London: Soncino, 1947), p. 64.

[7]See Nahum Sarna, *Understanding Genesis* (New York: Schocken Books, 1966), pp. 116, 121-122.

[8]See *ANET*, p. 220. Less applicable is section 146 of the Code of Hammurabi (*ANET*, p. 172).

[9]Compare a law in the Ur-Nammu collection, in *ANET*, p. 525.

5

BIBLE VERSUS BABEL

Why Did God Tell Abraham to Leave Mesopotamia for the Backwater Region of Canaan?

JACOB MILGROM

Genesis 12 begins enigmatically: "The Lord said to Abram, 'Go forth from your land, and from your kin group, and from your father's house to the land that I will show you.'" Abraham was a native of Mesopotamia (present-day Iraq), the most advanced civilization of its time. Mesopotamia was known for its knowledge in the arts and sciences—mathematics, astronomy, architecture, irrigation and animal husbandry—and, above all, for its cities. Babylon, for example, comprised 2,500 acres, larger even than the 1,850 acres of Nineveh, a city that took three days to traverse (Jonah 3:3).

Babylon's population is estimated to have been 100,000, and the alluvial plain in which Babylon was situated (at the head of the

Persian Gulf) may have contained as many as a million people. Why then did Abraham leave, especially for the backwater region of Canaan? More precisely, why did God want him to leave? The answer must reside in the previous chapter, chapter 11. It is an anti-Babylonian polemic.

Note the mocking irony of the text: "Brick served them as stone, and bitumen served them as mortar" (Genesis 11:3). They used inferior materials! Instead of stone and mortar (plentiful in Canaan), they used brick and bitumen. They schemed to build a city and a tower "with its top in the sky" (Genesis 11:4)—a clear reference to Esagila, the famed ziggurat of Babylon, whose name means "the structure with the upraised head." Yet it did not reach the sky. To inspect the tower, "the Lord came down" (Genesis 11:5); and his divine agents were likewise instructed: "Let us go down" (Genesis 11:7).

The irony in the text is emphasized by key passages. The Babylonians wanted to build a city, "else we shall be scattered over the whole earth" (Genesis 11:4). The Lord, however, "scattered them over the face of the whole earth" (Genesis 11:8-9). Even the structure of this passage discloses its anti-Babylonian stance: Verses 1-4 declare the Babylonians' intention; verses 5-9 describe the intervention of the Lord. The second half completely reverses the first half. In other words, "man proposes and God disposes."

In the biblical view, humans were directed to "be fruitful and multiply, and fill the earth" (Genesis 1:28, 9:1). Instead, the Babylonians schemed: "Let us build us a city and a tower." To be sure, biblical criticism assigns Genesis 1 and 11 to different sources. But the redactor deliberately arranged these chapters in their present order. God countered the Babylonians' defiance; he "scattered them over the face of the whole earth" (Genesis 11:8,9). This episode betrays the anti-urban bias of the Bible. Babylonian cities were characterized by increasing congestion. But instead of building out, the Babylonians built up—a skyscraper (the tower). Urban blight and poverty set in, spawning lawlessness and street violence.

Mesopotamian religion was no help. Polytheism meant chronic indecision in heaven, and therefore chronic instability on earth. The city, with its endemic problems of congestion, pollution and moral decay, was hardly the environment for fostering the ethical life. Who founded the city, according to the Bible? Cain, the first murderer (Genesis 4:8,17). Moreover, it is no accident that the patriarchs of Genesis encamped near cities, presumably for commercial purposes, but never settled in them. Jacob is a striking example. He buys property outside Shechem (Genesis 33:19), and even after his sons Simeon and Levi sack the city and despoil it (Genesis 34:27-29), Jacob and his family do not occupy it.

Mesopotamian mythology confirms that solutions other than the biblical one were devised to reduce overpopulation. The creation myth of Atrahasis informs us that the gods attempted to curtail human population by a series of natural disasters. When these failed, the gods decided to eliminate the human race by a worldwide flood. Atrahasis, the Mesopotamian Noah, was saved through the intervention of his protector god. Finally, a compromise was reached that appeased the enraged gods. Henceforth, human population would be controlled not only by natural disasters but also by internal birth control: natural barrenness, high infant mortality and three orders of celibate priestesses.

It is thus no accident that Genesis 11 comes after the biblical flood story (Genesis 6-9). The Bible is saying: You Babylonians claim that the gods have solved the problem of overpopulation by instituting natural disasters and birth control. There is a better way: Break up your cities. They only spawn poverty and crime. "Fill the earth" (Genesis 9:1). Build out, not up.

We can now understand why God told Abraham to leave Mesopotamia: It is no place to raise a family. In a sense Abraham was a postdiluvian Noah. Abraham was to be saved from the moral corruption of Mesopotamia. He was destined to be the founding father of a people who would "follow the way of the Lord to act in righteousness and justice" (Genesis 18:19), setting an example for humanity to emulate. And thus through Abraham "all the families of the earth will be blessed" (Genesis 12:3).

Abraham was given a solution. But what will be ours—to move to the moon? I am sure that many readers have shared my experience of flying cross-country in the early evening hours and noticing that between brightly lit cities there are vast areas of total darkness. Is there still room to "fill the earth"?

Reprinted from Bible Review, *April 1995.*

6

THE BAPTISM
OF JESUS

*A Story Modeled
on the Binding of Isaac*

WILLIAM R. STEGNER

J ohn's baptism of Jesus appears in all three Synoptic Gospels (Matthew, Mark and Luke). Exegetes have puzzled for centuries over the theological meaning of Jesus' baptism, particularly as derived from Mark's account. Here is how Mark describes it in a mere 53 words in Greek:

> In those days Jesus came from Nazareth of Galilee and was baptized by John in the Jordan. And when he came up out of the water, immediately he saw the heavens opened and the Spirit descending upon him like a dove; and a voice came from heaven, "Thou art my beloved Son; with thee I am well pleased."
>
> Mark 1:9-11; see also Matthew 3:13-17, Luke 3:21-22

A new understanding emerges, I believe, when we realize that this baptism story was modeled on the Old Testament account of Abraham's near-sacrifice of his son Isaac, an episode known to students of the

Old Testament as the binding of Isaac. In the biblical form of the story (Genesis 22), God tests Abraham by telling him to take his only son Isaac and offer him to God as a sacrifice. Abraham takes his son to the mountain to which God directs them and prepares an altar on which he lays wood. Abraham then binds his son, lays him on the altar and raises his knife to slay him. At this dramatic moment an "angel of the Lord called to him from heaven" and tells Abraham to desist, "for now I know that you fear God, seeing you have not withheld your son, your only son, from me." Abraham "lifted up his eyes" and sees a ram caught in a thicket. Abraham then sacrifices the ram in place of his son Isaac.

At first glance, the stories of Jesus' baptism* and the binding of Isaac appear to have little relationship to one another. Let us look more closely, however.

The story of the binding of Isaac is told in Genesis 22. But it was such a powerful story that it was told and retold over the centuries in various versions from a variety of viewpoints and with a variety of embellishments. Indeed, this was true of much of the Old Testament. That is how the midrash developed. The midrash is a collection of retellings and elaborations of biblical stories written down beginning in about 400 C.E. Many of the exegetical traditions that the midrash embodies, however, were known much earlier.

Over the centuries Jewish exegesis and elaboration of Scripture occurred in many forms in addition to the midrash—forms we might call midrashic. The Targums, for example, are loose translations of the Hebrew scriptures—paraphrases might be a better word—into Aramaic, at a time when Aramaic was the everyday language of the people. The Targums often contain embellishments

---

*In Matthew and Luke, the account of Jesus' baptism immediately follows the account of his birth and infancy and is, in effect, introduced by the birth and infancy narratives. Mark does not contain a birth and infancy section: The story of Jesus' baptism in Mark therefore serves a somewhat different function and plays a somewhat different role.

to and explanations of the Hebrew scriptural text that are not found
in the original.

One of the most significant changes introduced into the biblical
account by later midrashic versions (including the Targums) concerns the role of Isaac, who plays an increasingly prominent part.
As one scholar has described the difference:

> In Genesis it is Abraham's faith and obedience to God's will even
> to the offering of his only son, the child of promise, that constitutes
> the whole significance of the story: Isaac is a purely passive figure.
> In the rabbinical literature, however, the voluntariness of the sacri-
> fice on Isaac's part is strongly emphasized.[1]

In the account in Genesis, the main character is Abraham; Isaac
seems to be a mere lad. According to one midrash, however, he was
37 years old.

The Targums survive, in part, in several manuscripts, known
to scholars as Targum Pseudo-Jonathan (also called Yerushalmi
I), Neofiti and the Fragmentary Targum (or Yerushalmi II).
Variations occur among the manuscripts, but the basic emphasis
on Isaac's willingness to be sacrificed is common to all of these
targumic manuscripts.

It is the targumic versions of the story of the binding of Isaac that
I believe served as a model for the story of the baptism of Jesus.*

---

*There is considerable scholarly debate about the date of the Targums. Although they
may have been edited and "published" considerably later than New Testament times
(some say as late as the seventh or eighth century C.E.), various passages in the Targums
obviously must be dated much earlier. This is true of the material relating to the binding
of Isaac. We have a number of clues suggesting that the targumic version of the story of
the binding of Isaac was well known in New Testament times. For example, the works of
Philo and Josephus and other first-century C.E. documents all describe the voluntary
nature of Isaac's submission to sacrifice. Even more significant is the fact that the targumic material locates the binding of Isaac on the Temple Mount in Jerusalem. In the targumic accounts, when Isaac looks up from the altar, he has a vision of God's glory known
in rabbinic literature as the Shekinah, which dwelt in the Temple. In this way the Targums
use the binding of Isaac to prove the sole legitimacy of Jerusalem and its Temple as the
place of sacrifice. This makes good sense only in the period before 70 C.E., before the
Roman destruction of the Temple, and suggests that those details were incorporated into
the story before the Temple's destruction.

Thus, a version of the Isaac story, now found in these Targums, must have been widely known when the story that lies behind the Gospel account of Jesus' baptism was composed.

When Jesus came out of the water after his baptism (plate 5, p. 81), the following things occurred (again I quote from Mark):

1. "He saw the heavens opened and the Spirit descend[ing] upon him."

2. "A voice came from heaven [and said], 'Thou art my beloved Son; with thee I am well pleased.'"

Each of these features of the baptism story finds its parallel in the targumic stories of the binding of Isaac.

1. As Isaac lay bound upon the altar, he too looked up and saw "the angels of the height."[2] He too had a vision and saw "the Shekinah [the divine essence or spirit] of the Lord."[3]

2. A voice from heaven explains the significance of the scene: "Come, see two chosen individuals in the world; the one sacrificing and the other being sacrificed; the one sacrificing is not hesitating and the one being sacrificed stretches forth his neck."[4]

Bible scholars would say that the two stories exemplify the same form, a form often used by biblical writers to describe a vision. When a vision is described, the narrative frequently mentions the opening of heaven or a voice from heaven. In the Targums, this literary form of the vision is retained, but greater stress is placed on the content of the heavenly words than is the case in the biblical visions. The heavenly words emphasize the significance of the moment for the life of the person who receives the vision.

In both the baptism story and the binding story, however, the voice from heaven describes the significance of the scene, in one instance for Jesus, and in the other for Isaac. Both accounts exemplify the same literary form, namely the Old Testament form of a vision providing interpretive words from heaven.[5]

The fact that both stories exemplify the same literary form is only the beginning; they have far more in common than this. *Within* this form we find additional striking similarities: Lying on the altar, Isaac looks up and sees "the angels of the height." This seems to be another way of saying that the heavens were opened, since in the ancient worldview God and his angels were to be found above the vault of the heavens. In the Gospel account, the heavens had to be "opened"* before the Holy Spirit could be seen.

More significant, the content of the vision is almost the same in both stories. In the Gospels, Jesus sees "the Spirit descending"; in the targumic accounts of the Genesis story, "the Shekinah of the Lord" is revealed to Isaac.

The similarity between the Spirit** and the Shekinah is obvious. The Shekinah, in rabbinic thought, is a manifestation of God himself, reflecting his nearness to his people.[6] In the Gospel accounts, the Spirit or Holy Spirit indicates the presence and nearness of God.

So close are the two terms—Shekinah and Holy Spirit—that in some texts they are used interchangeably. As one observer has commented:

> The two expressions are often interchanged in the old Rabbinic texts. Both are frequently used as synonyms for God ... The man who is closely united with the Shekhinah also possesses the Holy Spirit, and the one possessing the Spirit also sees the Shekhinah.[7]

Moreover, the words the heavenly voice addresses to Jesus have a direct relationship to the account of the binding of Isaac.

Says the heavenly voice: "Thou art my beloved Son; with thee I am well pleased."[†] In the Greek translation of the Bible known as the Septuagint, translated from the Hebrew about 300 B.C.E., Isaac is

---

*The Revised Standard Version says the "heavens opened"; a more accurate translation is that the heavens "split."

**In the parallel synoptic accounts, where Mark uses "Spirit," Luke uses "Holy Spirit" (Luke 3:22) and Matthew uses "Spirit of God" (Matthew 3:16).

†Some commentators suggest that the phrase "Thou art my beloved Son" is a quotation from Psalm 2:7, applied to Jesus by the heavenly voice. But the Psalm, referring to Israel's king, says "You are my son," not "You are my beloved son." The absence of "beloved" is a serious objection to this view.

referred to as "the beloved son." Thus the heavenly voice echoes the Greek translation of Genesis.

The second half of the message from the heavenly voice, "with thee I am well pleased," also finds an echo in the binding of Isaac. In effect, the heavenly voice tells Jesus that he is the recipient of God's "elective good pleasure."[8] The Greek word for "pleased" is *eudokeō*; it can also mean "choice," conveying the notion of election. The idea of election is found twice in the targumic accounts of the binding of Isaac. There the heavenly voice applies the Aramaic term for men elected by God (*yachida*) to both Isaac and Abraham.*

Another connection that has frequently been made between the two stories is that Isaac was a near-sacrifice, while Jesus, the lamb of God, was actually sacrificed.** In the Targums to Leviticus 22:27, Isaac is referred to as a "lamb who has been elected/chosen."

Thus, the concept of God's choice or election is found both in the story of Jesus' baptism and in the binding of Isaac.†

One of the most enigmatic details in the baptism story is the dove: "The Spirit descend[ed] upon [Jesus] like a dove."

Most commentators see the dove as a symbol of Israel. A beautiful midrash comments on the phrase from the Song of Songs 4:1,‡ "Thine eyes are as doves":

> As the dove is chaste, so Israel are [sic] chaste. As the dove puts forth her neck for slaughter, so do [sic] Israel, as it says, "For Thy sake we are killed all the day" [Psalm 44:23]. As the dove atones for iniquities, so Israel atone [sic] for the other nations.[9]

---

*Some commentators argue that the Gospel phrase "with thee I am well pleased" is a quotation from Isaiah 42:1. Again, however, the verb in Isaiah is different: "Behold my servant ... in whom my soul delights."

**See 1 Corinthians 5:7: "For Christ, our paschal lamb, has been sacrificed." In John 1:29 Jesus is referred to as the "Lamb of God."

†Unlike theories that attribute different parts of the heavenly voice in the baptism story to different parts of the Old Testament, the theory suggested here has the advantage of simplicity. Both parts of the statement are derived from the same story, the binding of Isaac.

‡Some Bibles, such as the popular Revised Standard Version, refer to the Song of Songs as the Song of Solomon, its traditional title, based on its customary attribution to Solomon. See Jack M. Sasson, "Unlocking the Poetry of Love in the Song of Songs," *Bible Review*, February 1985.

The dove shares a remarkable characteristic with Isaac: Both the dove and Isaac stretch forth their necks as sacrifices. As the Targums say: "Come, see two unique individuals [Abraham and Isaac] ... the one being sacrificed [Isaac] stretches forth his neck." Note the equation. The dove, a symbol for Israel, makes atonement and stretches forth the neck. Isaac, too, stretches forth his neck on the altar as he makes atonement for Israel. Could the dove, associated with Isaac in later rabbinic literature, have been already associated with him in New Testament times? Could the dove in the baptism story have been a reminder of the similar roles played by Isaac and Jesus? Here is another bridge between the figure of Isaac and the story of Jesus' baptism.

In short, the baptism story was told with the story of the binding of Isaac in mind, as suggested not only by the literary form the stories share, but also by direct similarities and echoes in content. The reader of the baptism story was supposed to recall the story of Isaac.

Telltale verbal similarities between Mark and the Septuagint translation of Genesis 22 also support this interpretation (a fact no other commentator seems to have noticed). Both stories begin with the same introductory phrase: "and it happened." (The Revised Standard Version omits this phrase in translating Mark 1:9.)

Again: Jesus "saw" the heavens "being split," while Abraham "saw" the place where he was to sacrifice Isaac. In Genesis 22:14, Abraham names the place "[The] Lord will see."

And while Jesus saw the heavens "being split," Abraham "split" the wood for the burnt offering. In Genesis 22:11 and 22:15, the voice calls to Abraham "from heaven" (singular); in Mark 1:11 a voice comes "from heaven" (plural). The cumulative effect of the verbal agreements within the short span of the baptism narrative is indeed remarkable.

The author modeled his story of the baptism of Jesus on the story of the binding of Isaac for a reason. He had a point to make, a theological point.

The theology of the targumic story of the binding of Isaac is plain. The sins of Israel were forgiven by the continual sacrifices offered in the Temple at Jerusalem. The near-sacrifice of Isaac was regarded as a kind of original sacrificial offering that validated and gave significance to all subsequent sacrifices offered on the same mountain.

The Targum is clear that Mt. Moriah, where the binding of Isaac occurred, was in fact the Temple Mount. The relationship between the near-sacrifice of Isaac and the regular sacrifices offered on the Temple Mount is reflected in Geza Vermes's beautiful translation of the Fragmentary Targum to Genesis 22:14:

> Now I pray for mercy before you, O Lord God, that when the children of Isaac come to a time of distress, you may remember on their behalf the binding of Isaac their father, and loose and forgive them their sins and deliver them from all distress, so that the generations which follow him may say: In the mountain of the Temple of the Lord, Abraham offered Isaac his son.[10]

The theological significance of the baptism story is not directly stated; hence, the confusion among contemporary interpreters. The theological significance is not directly stated, however, because the original hearers would have made the association with the Isaac story. Jesus is like Isaac, except that he was in fact sacrificed. They would have understood that the theology of the baptism story was the theology of the cross. Just as Isaac was offered as an expiatory sacrifice, so Jesus would be offered.

The theological point of the Isaac story dovetails with the theology of the cross. If the suggestion I am making is correct, the shadow of the sacrifice on the cross falls across the baptism story, which introduces the adult Jesus to the Gospel reader.

This suggestion is reinforced by the fact that two important words tie the baptism to the cross. The first is the word baptism itself.

In the third prediction of his suffering and death, Jesus, on the road to Jerusalem with his 12 disciples, foretells what will happen to him (Mark 10:32-34). James and John ask to sit at his right and left hand in his glory. Jesus replies:

> You do not know what you are asking. Are you able to drink the cup that I drink, or to be baptized with the baptism with which I am baptized?
>
> Mark 10:38

A second connection between Jesus' sacrifice on the cross and his baptism may be found in an occurrence described in a single word. As Jesus breathed his last on the cross, the curtain of the Temple was torn in two (Mark 15:37-38; Matthew 27:50-51). A more literal translation is "split" rather than "torn"; the Greek word is *schizō*.* The reader will recall that when Jesus came out of the water after being baptized, the heavens were opened (Mark 1:10; Matthew 3:16). Again, a more literal translation is "split" rather than "opened"; the same Greek word is used, *schizō*. In good rabbinic fashion, the scene of the baptism is tied to the scene of the cross by use of this unusual word.**

Jesus' baptism is thus connected both to his sacrificial death and to the story of the sacrificial binding of Isaac, on which the baptism story was modeled.

I do not mean to imply that this is the *only* correct interpretation of Jesus' baptism, but it is surely *one* valid interpretation. There probably is no single correct interpretation of the baptism story. There are probably layers of meaning in the story. The baptism story was doubtless formulated in the early Aramaic-speaking church. It is entirely consistent with the rabbinic Palestinian milieu that there should have been more than one proper interpretation

---

*For our purposes it does not matter whether the tearing of the curtain is a sign of God's judgment on the Temple or a sign that access to God is now open and visible as a result of the cross.

**This is a device known as *gazera shava*, which is an "analogy of expressions; that is, an analogy based on identical or similar words occurring in two different passages of Scripture" (M. Mielzinger, *Introduction to the Talmud* [New York: Bloch, 1968], p. 143). According to exegetical practice, if one of the passages in which the word occurs is obscure, its meaning is to be ascertained from the other passage.

of a story. What I have presented is simply what the rabbis would refer to as "another interpretation."
Reprinted from Bible Review, *Fall 1985.*

[1]G.F. Moore, *Jerusalem in the First Centuries of the Christian Era*, Vol. 1 (Cambridge, MA: Harvard University Press, 1932), p. 539.

[2]The three Targums to Genesis 22:10.

[3]Targum Pseudo-Jonathan to Genesis 22:14. The other two Targums, namely Neofiti and the Fragmentary Targum, use "the glory of the Shekinah of the Lord." There is little difference between these two expressions.

[4]The three Targums to Genesis 22:10.

[5]Here I am especially indebted to the analysis of Fritzleo Lentzen-Deis, *Die Taufe Jesu nach den Synoptikern* (Frankfurt am Main: Knecht, 1970), pp. 97-248.

[6]Ephraim E. Urbach, *The Sages—Their Concepts and Beliefs*, trans. from the Hebrew by I. Abrahams (Jerusalem: Magnes, 1975), p. 43. Also see the discussion by A. Unterman, *Encyclopedia Judaica*, Vol. 14, "Shekhinah" (Jerusalem: Keter, 1971), pp. 1350ff.

[7]A. Marmorstein, "The Holy Spirit in Rabbinic Legend," *Studies in Jewish Theology*, ed. J. Rabinowitz and M. Lew (Freeport, NY: Books for Libraries, 1972), p. 131.

[8]G. Schrenk, *Theological Dictionary of the New Testament*, ed. G. Kittel, Vol. 2 (Grand Rapids, MI: Eerdmans, 1974), pp. 740ff.

[9]Midrash *Rabbah*. Song of Songs, trans. M. Simon (London: Soncino, 1939), p. 86.

[10]Geza Vermes, *Scripture and Tradition in Judaism* (Leiden: Brill, 1973), p. 195.

7

THE STARS IN THE HEAVENS

Many or a Few?

L ook toward heaven and count the stars, if you are able to count them," the Lord told Abram in a vision. He then added, "So shall your descendants be" (Genesis 15:5). The Lord appeared to Isaac and told him, "I will make your descendants as numerous as the stars of heaven" (Genesis 26:4).

There is a problem with this oft-repeated and oft-referred-to divine promise. There really aren't that many stars in heaven that can be seen with the unaided eye. Astronomers tell us that without some form of telescope we can see only between 2,000 and 4,000 stars, even on a good night. That's not really that many descendants. A single generation of Hebrews no doubt exceeded this number at a very early point in their history.

Did the biblical writer think 4,000 was a lot? Or, as he looked into the heavens, did he estimate badly and fail to realize that the number of visible stars was quite limited? Perhaps it seemed to him that there were countless stars in the heavens even though in fact there were only, at most, 4,000 visible to his eyes.

Or perhaps there is another explanation—suggested by other verses in the Bible. Elsewhere in the Bible, the divine promise is expressed not only in terms of the number of stars in the heavens, but in terms of the sands on the seashore and the dust of the earth. Now here we are truly talking about big numbers.

For example, in Genesis 22:17 an angel of the Lord, speaking in the Lord's name, tells Abraham, "I will bestow my blessing on you and make your descendants as numerous as the stars of heaven and the sands on the seashore." In Genesis 28:14 the comparison is with the dust of the earth. The Lord tells Jacob, "Your descendants shall be as the dust of the earth."

Surely even a casual observer would know that the number of grains of sand on the seashore or particles of dust on the earth is far greater than the number of stars visible to the unaided eye. Why would the biblical writer make such a lopsided comparison? The divine promise was, on the one hand, comparatively quite small (the stars in heaven) and, on the other hand, enormous (the sands of the sea and the dust of the earth). But is the comparison really so lopsided? Or did the biblical writer know how many stars there actually are?[1]

In fact, there are billions of stars, not just 4,000.* But only recently has modern astronomy—with its powerful telescopes—discovered this. The biblical writer could not have known this.

Or could he? If he did, this would indeed have made the analogy to the stars quite apt, as it is for sand and dust. It would also make more sense to join the number of stars in the heavens to the number of sands by the sea or to the dust on the earth in the various statements of the divine promise.

---

*More precisely, astronomers estimate that there are about 40 billion trillion stars in the universe.

Josephus, the first-century C.E. Jewish historian, quotes a third-century B.C.E. Babylonian writer named Becosus to the effect that Abraham was an astronomer. According to Josephus, Becosus described Abraham as "a man righteous and great, and skillful in the celestial science."[2]

Is it possible that the biblical writer knew and Abraham understood that there were billions of stars? Could the ancients have had telescopes that revealed stars the naked eye could not see?

A rock-crystal lens found in the ruins of the treasure house at Nineveh suggests that they may indeed have known. Sir David Brewster, an authority on optics, made a careful examination of the lens and presented his findings to the British Association in 1852.[3] He said the lens had a planoconvex form (the reference says "concave" in one place and "convex" in another, but the latter appears to be correct). Experiments with polarized light showed that its plane face had been "one of the original faces of the six-sided crystal of quartz." The convex face had been shaped on a lapidary's wheel, or by some similarly crude method, which gave the lens an unequal thickness, with 0.2 inches as a maximum, and a focal length of 4.5 inches. The lens was also imperfectly circular across its faces, having diameters that ranged between 1.6 and 1.4 inches. These dimensions are similar to those of the lenses in Galileo's first telescope, but a second lens would have been necessary to achieve magnification. Sir David concluded that the crystal "could not be looked on as an ornament, but as a true optical lens."

This is not the only known ancient lens, however. In July 1930, the *British Journal of Physiological Optics* published a survey by H.L. Taylor on "The Origin and Development of Lenses in Ancient Times." As a result of his examination of lenses in eastern Mediterranean museums, including some "perfect lenses" found at Knossos and Mount Ida, Taylor attributed the development of lenses to the Cretans of 1800 B.C.E. Five glass lenses from Carthage are of particular interest, because two of them hint at a practical function. These two were discovered "in the sarcophagus of a prominent individual, who, it is presumed, suffered from presbyopia and wished to protect himself against this disability in his next existence."[4]

Although we have no definite evidence of how these lenses were used, we may wonder. Did the biblical writer make an inept comparison of the patriarch's descendants with the stars of the heavens, or did the biblical writer know long before modern science that there are, in fact, billions of stars?

Reprinted from Bible Review, *Fall 1987*

[1]This chapter was suggested by reader Bill Ickes of Berlin, Pennsylvania, who also supplied the biblical and other references. We are grateful to Dr. Kenneth Brecher, Department of Astronomy, Boston University, and to Dr. Roger A. Bell, professor of astronomy at the University of Maryland, for their comments and corrections.

[2]Josephus, *Antiquities of the Jews* 1.7.

[3]"On a Rock-Crystal Lens and Decomposed Glass Found in Nineveh," abstract in *The American Journal of Science and Arts*, May 1853, pp. 122-123.

[4]"Carthaginian Lenses," abstract in *Nature*, Sept. 13, 1930, p. 415.

II

SARAH
AND HAGAR

Sarah said to Abraham, "Cast out this slave-woman with her son; for the son of this slave woman shall not inherit along with my son Isaac."

GENESIS 21:10

8

HAGAR'S EXPULSION

A Tale Twice-Told in Genesis

ZEFIRA GITAY

T he artist is a biblical commentator just as surely as the literary critic who studies the Bible's internal devices, the form critic who looks at the origins of literary genres, or the source critic who tries to disentangle components that may have been woven together to create the text we know. Both artist and scholar alike face the Bible's complexity, which requires that they pick and choose among its myriad images, its contradictions and its obscure meanings.

The ancient text of the Bible, transmitted from generation to generation, inspired written works such as translations, commentaries, poetry and literature—and pictorial creations such as paintings, frescoes, mosaics and sculpture.

The medieval world recognized that both words and pictures served the same purpose—to communicate the Bible's message.

Pictures were treated as additional text, usually aimed at an audience not trained in the written word. Pope Gregory in the sixth century suggested that "painting can do for the illiterate what writing does for those who read."[1] And the 15th-century Dominican friar Savonarola wrote, "You fellow, ignorant of letters, go to the pictures and contemplate the life of Christ and his saints."[2] Words and pictures became interchangeable, and thoughts were recorded by one means or the other.

But there is a difference between writers and artists as they interpret the Bible. From one perspective the word is flexible and the picture is rigid. The writer has no limitations of time or space; the writer can move backward and forward in time and change locations at will. The artist chooses a defined space and time, which he or she can change only by working on a different surface. The artist cannot tell us about subtle thoughts and ideas with the limited vocabulary of pictographic symbols or with the words that may be inserted into that given space.

From another perspective—it is the painter who has the advantage. Leonardo da Vinci characterized the painter's advantage so eloquently that we must admire him not only as a pictorial artist, but as a master of words as well.

> If you, poet, describe a bloody battle, will it be with air dark and murky, in the midst of frightful and death-dealing arms, mixed with the thick dust that defiles the atmosphere and the frightened flight of miserable men afraid of a horrible death? In this case, the painter will surpass you because your pen will be worn out before you describe fully what the painter with his medium can represent at once. Your tongue will be paralyzed with thirst and your body with sleep and hunger, before you depict with words what the painter will show you in a moment.[3]

In biblical literature, the text is often skeletal. The literary critic Erich Auerbach observes that the Bible specifies "only so much of the phenomena as is necessary for the purpose of the narrative, all else is left in obscurity; the decisive points of the narrative alone are emphasized, what lies between is nonexistent."[4] As a result, the artist is left to fill the gaps in the narrative, a task shaped by the artist's own personality, tradition, knowledge, experience and surroundings.[5]

Approaching a biblical text the artist asks: Which details of the story will I include? Which exclude? Which characters will be emphasized? Which minimized or ignored completely? How will I imagine the setting, the dress, the architecture—all the details undescribed but necessary to re-creating a human scene?

The Bible includes many instances in which a particular story is repeated but with variations. Here, too, the artist must "interpret" and choose the episode to illustrate.

In this chapter, I will look closely at the way several artists portrayed the events following Hagar's pregnancy with Ishmael. The story is told twice—in Genesis 16 and Genesis 21.

In Genesis 16, Abram* is told by the childless Sarai** that he should take her maidservant Hagar as his concubine so that he may have a child. Abram heeds Sarai's request and Hagar conceives. When Hagar discovers that she has conceived, she despises the barren Sarai. Sarai then complains to Abram about Hagar's behavior. Abram responds to Sarai, "Do to her [Hagar] as it pleases you" (Genesis 16:6).

Sarai does indeed do something harsh to Hagar (although what she does is not revealed). Hagar responds by fleeing to the wilderness where the angel of the Lord finds her by a spring on the way to Shur. The angel tells Hagar to return to Sarai to await the birth of her son, who shall be called Ishmael. Furthermore, the angel predicts that Ishmael "will be a wild man; his hand will be against every man

---

*Abram does not become Abraham until Genesis 17:4-5, when God makes a covenant with Abram and marks the new relationship by a change of name. God says: "No longer shall your name be Abram [the exalted father], but your name shall now be Abraham." Abraham is here taken to mean "father of a multitude of nations."
**Sarai becomes Sarah in Genesis 17:15,16, when God tells Abraham (no longer Abram) that Sarah will be blessed with a son. "She shall be a mother of nations; kings of people shall be of her." Sarah, a variant of Sarai, means "princess."

and every man's hand against him" (Genesis 16:12). Hagar returns
home and bears her son, who is then named Ishmael by Abram, his
father. Abram is 86 years old when Ishmael is born.

The next episode, in Genesis 21, occurs *after* the birth of Isaac
to Sarah and of Ishmael to Hagar. The occasion is a feast to cele-
brate Isaac's weaning. Sarah observes that Ishmael, Isaac's older
half-brother and son of Hagar, scoffs at Isaac. Sarah asks Abraham
to "cast out this bondswoman and her son; for the son of this
bondswoman shall not be heir with my son, Isaac" (Genesis 21:10).
God, urging Abraham to overcome his reluctance to act against
Hagar and Ishmael, advises Abraham: "Whatever Sarah has said to
you, do as she tells you, for through Isaac shall your descendants
be named" (Genesis 21:12).

Giving them bread and water, Abraham sends Hagar and Ishmael
into the wilderness of Beer-Sheva where they wander until the water
is gone and the weak child can only lie on the ground and await
death. Hagar weeps in despair. God hears the voice of Ishmael, and
an angel of God calls to Hagar saying, "Fear not, for God has heard
the voice of the lad ... Arise, lift up the lad and hold him with your
hand, for I will make him a great nation" (Genesis 21:17-18). God
opens Hagar's eyes, and she sees a well. His life saved, Ishmael
lives to become an archer in the wilderness of Paran (and the ancestor of the Arab nations).

Despite the many similarities between the narratives of Genesis
16 and 21,[6] there are also many differences. The differences are not
only in small details, but also in the basic sequence of events that
precede or follow the birth of Ishmael. Consider, for instance, Hagar's
arrival in the desert. In chapter 16, Sarai is barren; Hagar is pregnant with Abram's son, as was requested by Sarai in order to give
her husband an heir. In chapter 21, the events begin after Sarah has
given birth to Isaac, whose playmate is Ishmael, Hagar's son. In
chapter 16, the pregnant Hagar flees to the desert on her own and
meets the angel near the spring. In chapter 21, the story varies;

THE ARTIST BECOMES A BIBLICAL COMMENTATOR, according to author Zefira Gitay, when he or she chooses what story to portray and how to portray it. In his etching Abraham Casting out Hagar and Ishmael, *Rembrandt van Rijn (1606-1669) gives Abraham and his household all the trappings of 17th-century wealth, but Hagar's misery and Sarah's gloating come across with timeless poignancy. Little Isaac stands in the shadow of the doorway, his round face impassive. Is he mourning the loss of his older brother/playmate, or wondering whether his father will be so hard-hearted about his welfare, or merely contemplating his new position as sole son and promised heir?*

Hagar is supplied with bread and water by Abraham before she is sent by him into the wilderness with Ishmael. There is no water in the desert, and the boy almost dies of thirst. As Ishmael weakens, Hagar moves a "bowshot" away so as to not witness his death; then the angel appears to her, and she sees the well.

Hagar's flight also differs in the two scenes. In chapter 16, Sarai asks Abram's help in her rivalry with Hagar, but Abram refuses to interfere in his wife's affairs. Since Hagar is the maid, she is Sarai's responsibility;[7] Abram lets Sarai decide what to do. In chapter 21, Sarah asks Abraham to send the maid away; Abraham fulfills her request with regret, but nonetheless sends Hagar and Ishmael away.

When artists transformed the stories about Ishmael and Hagar into visual images, did they prefer the tale told in chapter 16 or the one related in chapter 21? Or did they intermingle the texts?

A close study of many artistic works that present Hagar reveals that the two episodes were not treated equally by artists. Most preferred to illustrate chapter 21. The artistic conceptions of chapter 21 usually combine the first two scenes of the text, in which Abraham sends Hagar and Ishmael away, having provided them with bread and water for the harsh journey, while in the background Sarah and her small son Isaac watch the event for which they are blamed. These episodes from chapter 21 of the biblical text have been depicted by such artists as Rembrandt (p. 77) and Gustave Doré (p. 88). Regardless of technique or style, the artists included in their pictures the literary details of the chapter 21 narrative. Often, all the characters of the story are included: Abraham, who feels sorrow at the need to send away his son Ishmael with Hagar; the rival female, Abraham's wife Sarah, who watches her husband so that he will not give in to his feelings and reverse his decision; and Isaac, Sarah's son, who will carry the blessing.

Plate 1 (top), The Binding of Isaac, *a floor mosaic from the Beth Alpha syna-gogue in Israel, and Plate 2 (bottom),* The Sacrifice of Isaac, *a fresco from the Priscilla Catacomb in Rome, depict the central event in the lives of Abraham and Isaac, known in Hebrew as the* Akedah *(Genesis 22:1-18). All of the stories in this book unfold beneath the shadow of this chilling—and foundational—event. In Chapter 1 Robin Jensen discusses the role of the* Akedah *in Judaism and Christianity: In Jewish tradition, the binding of Isaac expresses God's intention to have mercy on his people and his condemnation of child sacrifice. In Christianity, it prefigures the crucifixion.*

SCALA/ART RESOURCE, NY

REBECCA·DAT·POTŪ·SERV̄·O·ABRAHE·7·CAMELIS·SVIS·

SCALA/ART RESOURCE, NY

Plate 3 (top), Scenes from the Life of Abraham, a wall mosaic from the Church of San Vitale, in Ravenna, Italy, shows the promise given (at left, Sarah overhears the angel tell Abraham that she will give birth to a son; Genesis 18:10) and the promise threatened (Abraham raises the knife to kill Isaac; Genesis 22:10). In Plate 4 (bottom), Rebekah at the Well, a mosaic from the Cathedral of Monreale, Sicily, Abraham's servant meets the wife meant for Isaac (Genesis 24:15-20) so that the story, and the promise, can continue into the next generation. In Chapter 4 Larry Helyer describes this meeting as the resolution of Abraham's final crisis "on the bumpy road to fulfilling God's promise of an heir."

Plate 5. The Baptism of Christ. *Jesus is washed by the waters of the Jordan while John the Baptist reaches out to him from the shore, in this mosaic from the Church of San Marco, in Venice. In the same moment the heavens open, a dove descends and three angels lean toward Jesus. In Chapter 6 William Stegner points out parallels with the* Akedah *and suggests that the story of Jesus' baptism (Matthew 3:13-17; Mark 1:9-11; Luke 3:21-22) was modeled on the Old Testament account of the sacrifice of Isaac (Genesis 22:1-18).*

ERICH LESSING

Plate 6. The Sacrifice of Isaac. *Abraham turns his anguished face aside and holds the knife against his son's bare neck in this 15th-century sculpture by Donatello and Nanni di Bartolo. Is Abraham hesitating, playing for time and trusting that God will intervene, as Lippman Bodoff suggests in Chapter 2? After all, God did intervene to protect Abraham's first son, Ishmael, when he was cast out into the wilderness with his mother, Hagar (see the chapters by Zefira Gitay, Curt Leviant and Jonathan Kirsch). Or is Isaac just another pawn in the struggle between God and Abraham, as Philip Davies argues (Chapter 3)?*

Plate 7. Jacob Wrestling with the Angel. *The chapters in Part 4 focus on the third generation of Abraham's family: the family of Jacob. Jacob's life was one of conflict—with his brother, with his father-in-law, between his wives, among his sons, with his neighbors. Odilon Redon (1840-1916) painted Jacob's wrestling match on the bank of the Jabbok River (Genesis 32:24-32), a conflict from which Jacob emerged wounded but wiser and newly named "Israel." In Chapter 11 Elie Wiesel wonders why Jacob's brother Esau receives so little sympathy; Jack Miles suggests that Esau may be Jacob's wrestling partner (Chapter 12); and Carl Evans and Richard Elliott Friedman discuss Jacob's character—is he an "innocent man" or a deceiver (Chapters 13 and 14)?*

BROOKLYN MUSEUM OF ART

Plate 8. Rachel Hides the Teraphim. *Rachel steals her father's household gods when Jacob leaves Laban's home in Haran with his family and flocks. But Laban pursues them, and when he catches up with them, he searches the camp (Genesis 31:33-35). Giovanni Battista Tiepolo painted Rachel sitting on the saddlebag containing the idols, with Joseph at her knee and the other women and children of the family to the right. In Chapter 15 Gordon Tucker discusses Jacob's hasty curse, which means death for the person who stole the idols (Genesis 31:32); in Chapter 16, Samuel Dresner discusses Rachel and Leah's troubled relationship.*

Plate 9. Jacob Weeping over Joseph's Coat. *Marc Chagall (1887-1985) captures Jacob's despair over the apparent loss of Joseph as his other sons attempt to comfort him, knowing that their act is a deception: They have sold their annoying brother into slavery and hope never to see him again (Genesis 37:31-35). As Richard Elliott Friedman explains in Chapter 14, deception marked Jacob's life, and only when Joseph forgives his brothers will the cycle be broken.*

Plate 10. Jacob Blesses Joseph's Sons *in Rembrandt van Rijn's painting of the final episode in the patriarch's troubled life (Genesis 48:17-20). Gordon Tucker (Chapter 15) suggests that Jacob adopted Joseph's two sons to make amends for causing the death of Joseph's mother, Rachel. As if to perpetuate the sibling rivalry that plagued his own family, Jacob reaches over Manasseh to give the chief blessing to Ephraim, Joseph's younger child. And so the story continues.*

Some of the artists who illustrated this particular episode of Hagar's expulsion also inserted into it their version of a future event suggested by the end of chapter 21: In verse 20, the biblical narrator says of Ishmael: "And God was with the lad, and he grew; and he dwelt in the wilderness, and became an archer." In Rembrandt's etching of the departure of Hagar and Ishmael (p. 77), he equipped the boy with a quiver of arrows and a bow, as if to hint to the audience the outcome of the story.

The biblical text is not explicit about Ishmael's age,* nor about how he behaved at the moment when he and his mother were sent away by Abraham. The boy is usually portrayed as a youngster. He is envisioned either as a free-spirited child not participating in the events but playing with his bow and arrow, or as a participant sharing the burden of preparations for the journey by carrying the bread or guiding the animal. Some artists anticipate the boy's later emotions in their representations of Ishmael; for instance, Doré's etching (p. 88) depicts Ishmael's fear as he clings tightly to his mother's dress.

But not all of the artistic compositions were inspired by the rich narrative of Genesis 21. Some, such as the drawing by Rembrandt (p. 89), follow the account found in chapter 16. Here, Rembrandt illustrates Sarai's complaint to Abram that Hagar despises and scorns her. Abram does not interfere with his women and gives Sarai freedom to act according to her own judgment in regard to her pregnant maid Hagar. In Rembrandt's drawing, Sarai, the mistress of the house, turns to her husband, Abram. Abram turns away from Sarai and does not even glance at Hagar, the future mother of his son, as if to indicate that it is the responsibility of Sarai to deal with the rebellious pregnant maid, who has lost respect for her barren mistress.[8]

*Scholars calculate that because Abraham was 86 when Ishmael was born (Genesis 16:16) and 100 years old when Isaac was born (Genesis 21:5), Ishmael was in his teens (about 17) when he was sent into the wilderness at the time of Isaac's weaning (when Isaac would have been a toddler).

DOVER PICTORIAL ARCHIVE SERIES

*THE EXPULSION OF ISHMAEL AND HIS MOTHER by Gustave Doré
(1832-1883). In this illustration of Genesis 21, Abraham stands in front of his
tent, holding a shepherd's crook. In the background, the sheep sleep and Sarah
cradles the infant Isaac in her arms as if to protect him from interlopers. In the
foreground, Ishmael clings to Hagar, evidently terrified by Abraham's stern face
and the fearful journey ahead.*

HAGAR EAVESDROPS from behind a curtain, but we know it won't do her any good. Rembrandt's Sarah, Hagar and Abraham, *which depicts Genesis 16, shows Abraham listening—or, perhaps, not listening—to Sarah's complaint that Hagar, pregnant with Abraham's child, now scorns her barren mistress. Abraham won't interfere with Sarah's plan to punish Hagar, even though it endangers his unborn child.*

When artists have focused on Hagar, most often they choose to depict her actions as they are described in chapter 21: her confrontation with Sarah and her encounter with the angel of God in the desert. The most frequently represented scene is that of Hagar and Ishmael from chapter 21, rather than the solitary Hagar of chapter 16. For instance, the 19th-century French painter Jean Baptiste Corot depicts the desperate mother praying in the desert for her son's survival, as does Doré in a second engraving (p. 90). In other

AN INTENSE GRIEF suffuses Gustave Doré's Hagar and Ishmael in the Wilderness, *a wrenching depiction of Genesis 21:15-17. The empty water jug is cast aside, and Hagar, unwilling to look on the death of her child (who lies flat on the ground as if already dead), cries out in despair. We know that in a moment an angel will answer her and point out a well, unimaginable in Doré's rocky barren scene.*

90

works, artists dwell on the angel's miraculous discovery of the mother and son. Benjamin West, the 19th-century American artist, painted the angel pointing toward the source of life, the well. The 17th-century artist Francesco Cozza did not let Hagar wait for help, but portrayed her taking an active role in searching for the well. Cozza painted the angel appearing behind her and guiding her to the well. The motifs of life and death, the relationship between the suffering child and his desperate mother, the loneliness of the wilderness and the miracle of salvation have all been illustrated by artists.

Although some artists concentrated on Hagar in the desert, where, for an instant, she became the heroine, others, like Rembrandt, carefully portrayed both episodes in Genesis, focusing on one account at a time and faithfully adhering to it. The close study of biblical art may help us become aware of details in biblical texts and of nuances in the characters and emotions of the people engaged in biblical events.

Reprinted from Bible Review, Winter 1986.

[1] Beryl Smalley, *The Study of the Bible in the Middle Ages* (Notre Dame, IN: Notre Dame Univ., 1978), p. 86.

[2] Robert J. Clements, *Michelangelo's Theory of Art* (New York: Gramercy, 1961), pp. 80-81.

[3] Leonardo da Vinci, *Treatise on Painting* (Princeton, NJ: Princeton Univ. Press, 1956), Vol. 1, p. 30.

[4] Erich Auerbach, *Mimesis,* trans. Willard R. Trask, (Princeton, NJ: Princeton Univ. Press, 1953), p. 11.

[5] William Purcell, *Behold My Glory* (New York: Hawthorn Books, 1947), p. 11.

[6] Gerhard von Rad, *Genesis* (London: SCM, 1972), pp. 234-235.

[7] John Skinner, *Critical and Exegetical Commentary on Genesis* (Edinburgh: T & T Clark, 1969), p. 285. In early Mesopotamian and Egyptian law, wives had slaves who were their own property; the slave could not be the husband's concubine without the mistress's permission.

[8] Skinner, *Critical and Exegetical*, p. 286. When Hagar was pregnant with Abram's child she was no longer under Sarai's complete control, but, nevertheless, Abram puts Hagar back in her mistress's hands.

III

ISAAC
AND ISHMAEL

God said to Abraham, "Do not be distressed because of the boy and because of your slave woman ... For it is through Isaac that offspring shall be named for you. As for the son of the slave woman, I will make a nation of him also, because he is your offspring."

GENESIS 21:12-13

9

PARALLEL LIVES

The Trials and Traumas of Isaac and Ishmael

CURT LEVIANT

I saac and Ishmael are very different men. Indeed, the contrast between Isaac, the beloved son of Abraham, and his half-brother seems to dominate many aspects of their relationship. Yet both of Abraham's sons endure a strikingly similar life—indeed a near-death—experience. Is the Bible trying to tell us something with this little-noticed parallel?

Beginning with their births, the biblical account repeatedly draws out the *dissimilarities* between Abraham's sons. Isaac, we read, is born to the patriarch's wife Sarah; Ishmael, to Sarah's Egyptian maid, Hagar, whom Sarah had given to Abraham as a wife. As the boys grow, the contrast in their personalities becomes increasingly apparent. Ishmael, God tells Hagar, will be a "wild ass of a man," with "his hand against everyone and everyone's hand against him" (Genesis 16:12). After being cast out of Abraham's home, Ishmael is raised in the wilderness, where he becomes an archer; his wife, like his mother, is Egyptian (Genesis 21:20-21).

Isaac, on the other hand, is reared in the family home in Beer-Sheva. A successful farmer, he marries his cousin Rebekah. It is through Isaac, the younger son, that God's covenant with Abraham will be passed on: God promises Abraham that Sarah (not Hagar) will "give rise to nations; rulers of peoples shall issue from her" (Genesis 17:16).

Yet a parity at one point in their lives—indeed the seminal experience in both their lives—suggests that their stories might not be as different as they seem. Not even the midrash, usually so astute in detecting biblical parallels, has taken notice of the similarities in deed and wording in the texts describing Ishmael and Isaac on the brink of death.*

Late in life, having borne no children, Sarah sends her maid Hagar to Abraham as a co-wife.** Filled with jealousy when Hagar becomes pregnant, Sarah—with Abraham's consent—treats her maid harshly, and Hagar escapes to the wilderness (Genesis 16:1-6). Only when God intervenes does Hagar return to give birth to Ishmael. Fourteen years later, through divine intervention, Sarah herself becomes pregnant at age 90 and gives birth to Isaac.

The most famous episode in Isaac's life is known in Hebrew as the *Akedah*, or binding of Isaac, which Christians refer to as the sacrifice of Isaac (although no sacrifice actually takes place). The powerful, primal account of Isaac's near sacrifice (Genesis 22:1-19) has achieved mythic proportions. Not only is this story recited daily by Jews during the morning service, but many tragic events in Jewish history—the massacres during the Crusades, the pogroms in eastern Poland and the Ukraine in 1648 and 1649, the Russian pogroms of the late 19th century, and even the Holocaust—have been viewed through the prism of the *Akedah*.

---

*The midrash *Genesis Rabbah* 84:6, for example, notes the affinities between Jacob and Joseph.
**Although many translations use the term "concubine," the Hebrew has the word *isha* (Genesis 16:3), which means "wife," rather than *pilegesh*, which means "concubine."

Like Isaac, Ishmael, too, is brought to the brink of death and then miraculously saved.* Ishmael's near-death experience, recounted just one chapter earlier, in Genesis 21, also begins with a message from God to Abraham. This time, the divine voice tells the reluctant patriarch to obey Sarah's instructions to cast out Hagar and Ishmael.** Early the next morning, Abraham sends the mother and child away with only bread and water. Cast out, they wander in the wilderness of Beer-Sheva until their water runs out.

Not wanting to watch Ishmael die, Hagar sits apart from her son, weeping, until she is arrested by the voice of an angel crying, "What troubles you, Hagar? Fear not!" When she opens her eyes, she finds before her a well of water, which heralds the survival of mother and child.

On an emotional level, the two accounts are remarkably different. Ishmael's story is replete with feeling. We find Hagar desperately mourning what she sees as the inevitable loss of her only son. In Isaac's story, however, there is not one iota of fatherly compassion (nor are we given Sarah's reaction to the fate of her only son). Before the sacrifice, Abraham displays no regret, only blind obedience to God's will. And when Isaac is saved, Abraham expresses neither joy nor relief. The very man who showed compassion for the men of Sodom (Genesis 18:17-33), whom he did not even know, betrays no sympathy for his own favorite son; the man who was willing to bargain with God to save those strangers in Sodom and Gomorrah makes no effort to negotiate over Isaac's fate.

But despite these differences in tone, a close comparison of Ishmael's tale and the *Akedah* reveals that the biblical author selected

*In some Islamic traditions, it is Ishmael, not Isaac, who is bound to the altar.
**This is the second time Hagar leaves Abraham's home; the first occurred when she was pregnant with Ishmael. On Sarah's motives in casting out Hagar, see the next chapter, "What Did Sarah See?" by Jonathan Kirsch.

his words to draw out the parallels between the two incidents and to present Ishmael's suffering as a parallel *Akedah*.

The affinity of the two sons is first highlighted by the use of similar expressions and the same word order in recording their births:

Isaac (Genesis 21:2-3)	*Ishmael* (Genesis 16:15)
"Sarah bore Abraham a son in his old age, and Abraham gave the son ... that Sarah bore him the name Isaac."	"Hagar bore Abram a son, and Abram gave the son that Hagar bore the name Ishmael."
"Va-teled Sarah le-Avraham ben le-zekunav, va-yikra Avraham et shem b'no ... asher yaldah lo Sarah, Yitzchak."	*"Va-teled Hagar le-Avram ben, va-yikra Avram shem b'no asher yaldah Hagar, Yishmael."*

Both of the *Akedah* stories begin with God telling Abraham to take action regarding his son:

Isaac (Genesis 22:2)	*Ishmael* (Genesis 21:12)
"He [God] said [to Abraham], take your son ... and offer him there as a burnt offering on one of the heights that I will tell (*omar*) to you."	"God said to Abraham ... [do] whatever Sarah will tell (*omar*) to you, listen to her voice."
"Va-yomer kach et bincha ... asher omar elecha."	*"Va-yomer Elohim ... kol asher tomar elecha Sarah, shma b'kolah."*

The future tense of the Hebrew verb "to tell" (*omar*) is used in both. Identical words initiate the action in both accounts:

Isaac (Genesis 22:3)	*Ishmael* (Genesis 21:14)
"Abraham arose early in the morning."	"Abraham arose early in the morning."
"Va-yashkem Avraham ba-boker."	*"Va-yashkem Avraham ba-boker."*

Upon rising, Abraham gathers the participants and the implements associated with each *Akedah*. He places the wood on Isaac and the bread, water and child on Hagar. The verbs for "take" and "put" are repeated in each story:

Isaac (Genesis 22:3,6)
"He [Abraham] took (va-yikach) ... Isaac ... and split the wood for the burnt offering ... Abraham took the wood for the burnt offering and put it on his son Isaac."

"Va-yikach ... et Yitzchak ... va-yevaka atezey olah ... Va-yikach Avraham et atzei ha-olah va-yasem al Yitzchak."

Ishmael (Genesis 21:14)
"He [Abraham] took (va-yikach) bread and a jug of water ... and put them on her [Hagar's] shoulders, together with the child."

"Va-yikach lechem ve-chemat mayim va-yiten el Hagar sam al shichmah ve-et ha-yeled."

Whereas wood and fire are key to the sacrifice in the Isaac story, it is the polar opposite of fire—water, and the lack thereof—that is the potential cause of death in the Ishmael account. So we see Abraham splitting wood for the sacrificial fire in the Isaac scene and, in the Ishmael story, carrying the jug of water that will soon run out. Both stories use the same Hebrew verb, va-yikach (took), to show Abraham grasping the object that symbolizes the "sacrifice" of each son. In both stories, Abraham puts (yasem and sam) the objects—wood for Isaac, the water jug for Ishmael—on or near the intended victim. Further, in both stories, the verb "to go" (HLK) is used to describe getting to the place where the near sacrifices will occur:

Isaac (Genesis 22:3)
"He went (va-yelech)* to the place which God had told him."

"Va-yelech el ha-makom asher amar lo Elohim."

Ishmael (Genesis 21:14)
"She went (va-telech) and wandered in the wilderness of Beer-sheba."

"Va-telech va-teta be-midbar Be'er Shava."

Isaac travels with his father to the mountain, which proves to be a life-threatening destination for the child; Ishmael accompanies his mother to the desolate desert.

*Va-yelech is the third-person masculine form of HLK, "to go"; va-telech is the feminine form.

The next scene describes the preparations for death:

Isaac (Genesis 22:9-10)

"He [Abraham] bound his son Isaac and put him on the altar ... Abraham sent forth (*va-yishlach*) his hand and took the knife to kill his son."

"*Va-ya'akod et Yitzchak b'no va-yasem oto al ha-mizbe'ach ... va-yishlach Avraham et yado. Va-yikach et ha-ma'achelet lishchot et b'no.*"

Ishmael (Genesis 21:15)

"She [Hagar] cast (*va-tashlech*) the child under one of the bushes."

"*Va-tashlech et ha-yeled tachat achad ha-sichim.*"

In both stories the parent picks up the child. Hagar then throws (*va-tashlech*) her son under a bush; Abraham binds his son and then sends forth (*va-yishlach*), or raises, his hand. Although the verbs have two different roots, they have similar sounds and convey the sense of sending something forward and away—of casting off.[1]

Both stories also describe the place where the boy will die as "afar" (*RḤK*):

Isaac (Genesis 22:4)

"He saw the place from afar (*rachok*)."

"*Va-yar et ha-makom me-rachok.*"

Ishmael (Genesis 21:16)

"She sat down far away (*harchek*), a bowshot away."

"*Va-teshev la mi-neged harchek ki-m'tachavey keshet.*"

In the nick of time, salvation comes. An angel calls to each of the parents:

Isaac (Genesis 22:11)

"An angel of the Lord called to him [Abraham] from heaven."

"*Va-yikra elav mal'ach YHWH min ha-shamayim va-yomer.*"

Ishmael (Genesis 21:17)

"An angel of God called to Hagar from heaven."

"*Va-yikra mal'ach Elohim el Hagar min ha-shamayim va-yomer.*"

In both stories the phrasing is the same, except that "Lord" ("YHWH," the personal name of the Israelite God) is used in Isaac's story and "God" (the generic term "Elohim") in Ishmael's.

Immediately before or after the angels' calls, the parents' actions involve the verb NS', "to raise" or "to lift":

Isaac (Genesis 22:13)

"Abraham raised (*va-yisa*)* his eyes."

"*Va-yisa Avraham et enav.*"

Ishmael (Genesis 21:16)

"She [Hagar] raised (*va-tisa*) her voice."

"*Va-tisa et kolah.*"

The ordeal is now over; the threat of death is gone. Speaking to the parents, each angel uses the words "fear," "listen," "God" and "voice." In the Isaac story, Abraham listens to—that is, obeys—God; in the Ishmael story, God listens to Ishmael:

Isaac (Genesis 22:12,18)

"For you are God-fearing ... because you have listened to my voice."

"*Ki yere Elohim atah ... ekev asher shamata be-koli.*"

Ishmael (Genesis 21:17)

"Fear not, for God has listened to the voice of the boy."

"*Al tir'i ki shama Elohim et kol ha-na'ar.*"

In saving the boys, each angel uses the words "hand" and "boy":

Isaac (Genesis 22:12)

"Do not raise your hand against the boy."

"*Al tishlach yadcha el ha-na'ar.*"

Ishmael (Genesis 21:18)

"Lift up the boy and hold him by the hand."

"*Se'i et ha-na'ar ve-hachaziki et yadech bo.*"

In the next verse, along with salvation, comes the alternative to death. A ram serves as a substitute sacrifice for Isaac, and water saves Ishmael from death by dehydration:

Isaac (Genesis 22:13)

"Abraham raised his eyes and he saw a ram, caught in the thicket by its horns.

Ishmael (Genesis 21:19)

"Then God opened her eyes and she saw a well of water. She went (*va-telech*) and filled the

Va-yisa is the third-person masculine, *va-tisa* the third-person feminine of NS'.

So Abraham went (va-yelech) and took the ram and offered it up as a burnt offering in place of his son."

"Va-yisa Avraham et enav va-yar ve-heeney ayil ... Va-yelech Avraham va-yikach et ha-ayil va-ya'alehu l'olah tachat b'no."

jug with water, and let the boy drink."

"Va-yifkach Elohim et eyneha va-tere be'er mayim ... Va-telech va-temaley et ha-chemet mayim va-tashk et ha-na'ar."

These verses highlight the word "eyes" (feminine, *eyneha*; masculine, *enav*) to make the point that Hagar and Abraham suddenly see before them something unexpected—the snared ram and the desert well. Both verses conclude with the parent "going" to save the child.

Once the children are secure, saved from their respective *Akedahs*, the angel relates God's blessing and promise of greatness for the children:

Isaac (Genesis 22:17)

"I will make your descendants numerous as the stars of heaven and the sands of the seashore."

"Ve-harba arbeh et zar'acha ke-kochvey ha-shamayim ve-chachol asher al s'fat ha-yam."

Ishmael (Genesis 21:18)

"I will make a great nation of him."

"Ki le-goy gadol asimenu."

There is a fascinating crisscrossing of blessings regarding Ishmael's posterity on one side and Abraham and Isaac's on the other. As if to further accent the equality of Ishmael and Isaac, an angel of the Lord earlier spoke the same words to Hagar—"I will make your descendants numerous" (Genesis 16:10)—that the angel now speaks to Abraham. And the promise of a "great nation" (*goy gadol*) that is made to Ishmael here and also earlier (Genesis 17:20) has previously been made to Abraham (Genesis 12:2 and 18:18) and will later be made to Isaac's son Jacob (Genesis 46:3). Continuing his remarks to Hagar, the angel (Genesis 16:10) uses the very same words, "they shall be too numerous to count" (*lo yisafar me-rov*), regarding Ishmael's descendants that Jacob uses in referring to God's promise to him (Genesis 32:13). Moreover, the phrase "multiply exceedingly" is used for both Abraham's posterity and for Ishmael's: "I will multiply thee exceedingly"—*ve-arbeh otcha bi-me'od me'od* (Genesis 17:2)—for Abraham; and "I will multiply him exceedingly"—*ve-hirbeiti oto bi-me'od me'od* (Genesis 17:20)—for Ishmael.

After both trials, the heroes settle down:

Isaac (Genesis 22:19)	*Ishmael* (Genesis 21:21)
"He [Abraham (and thus Isaac)] dwelled ... in Beer-sheba."	"He [Ishmael] dwelled in the wilderness of Paran."
"*Va-yeshev ... bi-ve'er shava.*"	"*Va-yeshev be-midbar Paran.*"

There is a double irony here. Ishmael, who nearly died of thirst in the wilderness, settles in the wilderness of Paran. Abraham, who was responsible for exiling Hagar and their son Ishmael to the wilderness of Beer-Sheva, where they nearly die, himself settles (presumably with Isaac) in that town.

It is interesting to note that Genesis 16, which focuses on the pregnant Hagar's flight from Sarah's harsh treatment, serves as a prelude to the later event, when Hagar goes into the wilderness with her son, Ishmael. The mention of the desert and the wellsprings (Genesis 16:7) in the earlier story adumbrates Ishmael's future desert-and-water *Akedah*. When she hears the angel in the desert the first time, Hagar calls out, *atah el ro'ee*, "You are El-roi," or "You are God of seeing" (Genesis 16:13). She names the well *Be'er la-chay ro'ee*, "The well of the Living One who sees me" (Genesis 16:14). Following the near sacrifice of Isaac, Abraham, upon hearing the angel's voice, calls the place *Ha-shem yir'eh*, "The Lord will see" (Genesis 22:14). In both instances, the parents name the site where they hear the angel by including a name of God linked with the verb "see."

Many years later, having survived their traumatic experiences, both Ishmael and Isaac die peacefully in old age. As a final parallel, their deaths are described in identical words:

Isaac (Genesis 35:29)	Ishmael (Genesis 25:17)
"Isaac expired and died and was gathered unto his kin."	"He [Ishmael] expired and died and was gathered unto his kin."
"Va-yigva Yitzchak va-yamot, va-ye'asef el amav."	*"Va-yigva va-yamot, va-ye'asef el amav."*

The striking correspondences in the deeds and the very words of the Abraham–Isaac and Hagar–Ishmael stories are too numerous to be coincidental. And even more parallels may be cited: Both sons are circumcised (Genesis 17:25, 21:4). The parents of both "take" wives for their sons: Hagar for Ishmael (Genesis 21:21) and Abraham for Isaac (Genesis 24:3-4). And aside from similar general blessings, the specific number of 12 sons is used for Abraham's descendants (Jacob as father of 12 sons, Genesis 35:23) and for Ishmael's (Genesis 17:20 and 25:13-16).

The placement of the Ishmael–Hagar and Isaac–Abraham dramas in two contiguous chapters is no chance occurrence. Remarkably, too, both chapters, both *Akedahs*, are read in the synagogue on Rosh Hashanah as part of that holiday's Torah readings. The Ishmael–Hagar story (Genesis 21:1-34) is read on the first day of Rosh Hashanah, and the Isaac–Abraham narrative (Genesis 22:1-24) is read on the second.

Clearly, Ishmael's sufferings are intended as an analogue tragedy to the *Akedah* of Isaac, or as a parallel *Akedah*, perhaps to show the parity between the two sons of Abraham.

It is, of course, easier to find parallels than to explain why they exist, to impute motives to the biblical text. But the many parallels in events and wording give us a double focus. On the one hand they elevate, it would seem, the importance of Abraham as the father of not one but two peoples. After all, his two most important progeny, Isaac and Ishmael (whose names bear the roots "laugh" [*ZCHK*] and "hear" [*SHM'*]—two verbs that reverberate throughout Abraham's lifetime), are both saved from their trials and are blessed with many descendants.

This close parallel reading also reveals how unsparing the Bible is of its heroes' flaws. From the patriarchs through Moses, Aaron and David, the Bible does not cover up the leaders' moral lapses. As Abraham had no mercy vis-à-vis his son Isaac, but unquestioningly obeyed God's command, so did he mercilessly send out his other wife Hagar and son Ishmael into the desert to a sure death. In both instances, despite Abraham's lack of parental compassion, God rewards him. When we become aware of the parallels between Isaac and Ishmael and when we note Abraham's hand in both their lives, our reading of the first patriarch undergoes a subtle shift.

The careful construction of the boys' parallel lives shows that no matter how different they might seem at times, the two sons of Abraham are bound from birth to death by something more than brotherly kinship.

Reprinted from Bible Review, *April 1999.*

---

[1] The terms carry this meaning in several biblical passages. For *shlch* with a *chaf* as final letter, see Jeremiah 7:15, "And I will cast you out of My presence" (*Ve-hishlachti et chem me'al panay*) and Psalm 71:9, "Do not cast me off in old age" (*Al tashlicheni le-et ziknah*). For *shlch* with *chet* as final letter, see 2 Samuel 13:17, "Send that woman out of my presence" (*Shilchu na et zot me'alay ha-chutzah*) and Genesis 3:23, "The Lord God cast him out of the Garden of Eden" (*Va-yeshalichehu ... me-gan Eden*).

10

WHAT DID SARAH SEE?

JONATHAN KIRSCH

D id Ishmael, the firstborn son of the patriarch Abraham, molest his young half-brother, Isaac? The disappearance of four words in an early version of the biblical text raises the intriguing if troubling prospect that the Bible records an incident of incestuous child molestation, a notion so shocking that it may have been literally written out of the Bible by the rabbinic censors.

Abraham and Sarah are childless, as we read in Genesis, and so Sarah gives her handmaiden, an Egyptian woman named Hagar, to Abraham. Hagar eventually bears him a son, and Abraham names the boy Ishmael (Genesis 16:4-16).

As Ishmael is growing up, God makes a remarkable promise to the 99-year-old Abraham and his 90-year-old wife: Sarah will bear a son who will replace Ishmael as the inheritor of Abraham's divine blessing (Genesis 17:19). So remarkable is the news that Sarah laughs out loud; her son's name, Isaac, is a bit of Hebrew wordplay that means "I laughed" (Genesis 18:12, 21:3).*

And now the Bible presents a deeply enigmatic scene in which we find the teenage Ishmael at play with his little half-brother at a feast celebrating the fact that Isaac has been weaned from the breast (at last!). But the festivities are ruined for Sarah because she oversees Ishmael doing *something* to Isaac (Genesis 21:9), something so disturbing that Sarah promptly demands that Ishmael and his mother be cast out into the wilderness.

Exactly what does Sarah see, exactly what does Ishmael do, that prompts such anger and outrage in Sarah?

All we are told in some conventional English translations of the Bible is that Sarah sees Ishmael "mocking" young Isaac**—and we are asked to believe that thanks to a single adolescent taunt, Sarah drives mother and son into the desert to die.

Unless, that is, she saw something much worse.

A clue to the mystery of Sarah's murderous rage is to be found in the Hebrew word used in the Bible to describe what Ishmael does to Isaac: *t'sahak*.

One of the meanings of *t'sahak* is "laugh"—a play on Isaac's name (Yitzchak)—and that's the one on which translators, old and new, have relied, suggesting that Ishmael merely "mocked" or "laughed at" Isaac. What the translators are reluctant to let us know is that another meaning of *t'sahak* is "fondle" and that the original Hebrew text of the Bible may indicate that what Sarah actually saw was some sort of sex play between Ishmael and his little brother.

Indeed, the very same Hebrew word appears only a few lines later in Genesis to describe Isaac fondling Rebekah outside the window of Abimelech, king of the Philistines (Genesis 26:8).

*Or did she simply smile because she was so pleased at the news?—Ed.
**Other translations use "playing" rather than "mocking."

The mystery of what Sarah saw deepens when we notice that an entire phrase has been dropped from the passage in some versions of the Bible. The authoritative Hebrew text of the Bible—the Masoretic text—includes only a truncated description of what Ishmael is doing when Sarah sees him. "Sarah noticed that [Ishmael] was playing" (Genesis 21:9). But the early Greek version of the Bible (the Septuagint) and the Latin version (the Vulgate), both of which were translated from Hebrew manuscripts, some perhaps even more original than the Masoretic text, give the same verse as "Sarah noticed that [Ishmael] was playing *with her son Isaac.*"

What are we to make of the missing words in the Hebrew Bible? Some Bible critics have been bold enough to suggest that the pious editors of the Masoretic text sought to play down the disturbing sexuality of the scene by leaving out the key phrase "with her son Isaac." The Septuagint and the Vulgate, it is suggested, preserve the original, complete and unexpurgated text.[1]

The very suggestion that the Hebrew Bible masks an incident of incestuous child molestation is simply too hot for most scholars to handle. The rabbis explained away the whole episode by suggesting that Ishmael liked to play with a bow and arrows and "was in the habit of aiming his missiles in the direction of Isaac, saying at the same time that he was but jesting."[2] Even when some Bible commentators are willing to concede that "mocking" is not a justifiable translation of the Hebrew word, they still insist that the encounter between Ishmael and Isaac is wholly innocent: "His 'playing' with Isaac need mean no more than that the older boy was trying to amuse his little brother," wrote Ephraim Speiser, one of the most venerated modern Bible scholars. "There is nothing in the text to suggest that he was abusing him, a motive deduced by many troubled readers in their effort to account for Sarah's anger."[3]

But we might reach a different conclusion, if only out of regard for the simple human decency of the matriarch Sarah. After all, Hagar and Ishmael nearly perish in the wilderness. Unless we regard Sarah as so jealous of her son's birthright that she would literally kill for him—or as an out-and-out paranoid, as one Bible scholar has suggested[4]—then we must look for a more plausible explanation for her punishing rage than the mockery of a younger sibling by his older brother.[5] And the four words that have somehow disappeared from the Masoretic text of the Bible provide an intriguing explanation for what Sarah sees: Ishmael is taking a liberty with his little brother that his stepmother finds too shocking to tolerate.

Reprinted from Bible Review, *October 1998.*

[1] Gerald A. Larue, *Sex and the Bible* (Buffalo, NY: Prometheus, 1983), p. 99.

[2] Louis Ginzberg, *Legends of the Jews*, 7 vols. (Philadelphia: Jewish Publication Society, 1909-1938), vol. 1, p. 264.

[3] Ephraim A. Speiser, *Genesis*, Anchor Bible 1 (Garden City, NY: Doubleday, 1986), p. 155 n. 9.

[4] George W. Coats, "Lot," in *Understanding the Word*, ed. James T. Butler, Edgar W. Conrad and Ben C. Ollenburger (Sheffield: JSOT Press, 1985), p. 123.

[5] Larue, *Sex and the Bible*, p. 99.

IV
JACOB AND ESAU

When the boys grew up, Esau was a skillful hunter, a man of the field, while Jacob was a quiet man, living in tents. Isaac loved Esau, because he was fond of game; but Rebekah loved Jacob.

GENESIS 25:27-28

11

ESAU AND JACOB

ELIE WIESEL

At the risk of shocking my readers, I feel compelled to reveal my sympathy for a character that the Bible seems to treat rather badly. I am talking about Esau, the elder brother of Jacob. I feel sorry for him. I imagine him alone, always alone, bitter and unhappy. Except for his old father Isaac, blind and powerless, no one loves him. And his mother less than the rest of the world. Her mistrust of him is mixed with dislike. We can imagine her plotting against him. It is not surprising that Esau is rarely at home; perhaps he feels like an intruder there. The fields and forests are his kingdom.

Why does Rebekah loathe her older son? Even before giving him life, she resents him. Citing the sages, Rashi[1] gives us the answer: Pregnant with twins, Rebekah felt them stirring in different places inside her. When she passed before a house of study, Jacob wanted to come out. Before a place consecrated to idols, it was Esau who hastened to be born. Even in their mother's belly, they quarreled. Puzzled, Rebekah went to Shem in his yeshiva and asked him for an explanation. Shem predicted their future: One would be good, the other bad; each would found a nation, and the two would not be able to live together peacefully; when one nation ascended, the other would decline. So this is why Isaac's wife, deeply religious, favored her younger son. As did God. Does the Bible not say that "the older shall be servant to the younger?" (Genesis 25:23).

Poor Esau. He is not even born, and already he is persecuted, already he has been consigned to a wretched fate. All that he does, even the good, is construed badly.

JACOB TAKES ADVANTAGE of Esau's hunger and sells his older brother a bowl of lentils in exchange for his birthright. Elie Wiesel imagines Esau "alone, always alone, bitter and unhappy ... no one loves him." This drawing by Rembrandt expresses the artist's sympathy for the unloved Esau, who, like Ishmael, will be displaced by his younger brother. Bowl in hand, Esau faces the viewer across the table, his face lined with anxiety—or maybe hunger—while he shakes his brother's hand, cementing the deal. Jacob has his back to the viewer, perhaps shamed by driving such a hard bargain.

As the boys grow up, Esau loves to go out hunting while Jacob remains at home all the time. So what? Hunting isn't forbidden in the Bible. But the traditional commentaries, playing word games, reproach him with trickery, pretense, posing as a strictly pious man only to please his father.

Actually, Jacob seems the more cunning of the two. Did not Jacob persuade his older brother to sell his birthright for a simple bowl of lentils? Esau was famished, he was dying of hunger, and Jacob took advantage of it to trap him. If Esau hadn't been hungry, would he have accepted the trade?

Even worse: Jacob stole Esau's identity by presenting himself before their ailing father to receive the blessing intended for his older brother!

And if this wrong is not grievous enough, it was Esau's mother who was the instigator. It was her idea to play the trick of robbing Esau of what by right belonged to him. Jacob had only to follow her instructions. What to do, what to say, how to dress to fool Isaac: It was Rebekah who manipulated him. Did Esau know? And Isaac— did he suspect? He must have felt that something was wrong. Something must have bothered him, perhaps even distressed him, because the text says "*Vaye harad Yitzchak haradah gedolah,*" "And Isaac, filled with dread, was seized by a great trembling" (Genesis 27:33). The Tosaphists, early rabbinic scholars, give us this comment: Isaac trembled with fear twice in his life. The first time was at the *Akedah* (the binding), when he saw his father, knife in hand, ready to sacrifice him (Genesis 22). But now his fear was even more terrifying. He began to wonder about his own guilt, asking himself, What sin could I have committed that led me to bless my younger son before his brother?

We understand Esau's despair. He heaved a rending cry. Suddenly he must have understood the full measure of his tragedy: He was the victim of a family conspiracy. His brother's deceit was stronger than his father's ability to see through it. It was too late to set right what had been done, too late to repair the injustice.

What would Esau's response be? Would he now begin to despise his brother Jacob? Rebekah thinks so. The Scriptures do not. The biblical passage speaks only of Jacob's fear, but not of Esau's designs. For the commentators, however, they are overwhelming.

Meeting after a long separation, Esau embraces Jacob (Genesis 33:4). Perhaps he was emotionally moved, which would be natural. But the midrash claims that Esau's heart was not in it. Why not give him the benefit of the doubt? Where Esau is concerned, we always assume the worst.

Is Esau wholly innocent? If he is, Jacob would be wholly guilty. Neither is true. In claiming the blessing that belonged to the elder son, Jacob did not really lie. Had he not bought his brother's birthright from him? On the other hand, why did Isaac prefer Esau?

The story is complex enough. It becomes even more so when one recalls the traditional teaching that portrays Esau as Jacob's implacable enemy for all time. So Esau never overcame his anger.

The commentary of a great Hasidic master: The moment Esau discovered his betrayal by Jacob, he shed two tears. And it is because of those two tears that the Jewish people have shed so many tears during their exile.

But with all of that, we are the descendants and heirs of Jacob. And not of Esau.

Reprinted from Bible Review, *April 1998; Anne Renner, translator.*

---

[1]Rashi, a French Jew who lived from 1040 to 1105, wrote commentaries on almost every book of the Hebrew Bible and the Babylonian Talmud. The sages are earlier rabbinic authorities.

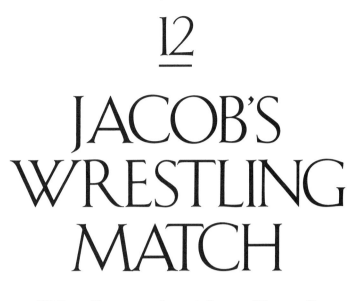

12

JACOB'S WRESTLING MATCH

Was It an Angel or Esau?

JACK MILES

n commenting on the story of Jacob and Esau, Elie Wiesel refers in passing to "the traditional teaching that portrays Esau as Jacob's implacable enemy for all time." The relevant verse in Genesis is 27:41, which comes just after Jacob has defrauded his brother of his inheritance: "*Wayyistom 'esaw 'et ya'aqob 'al habberakah*," translated in the King James Version, "And Esau hated Jacob because of the blessing."

The tradition that defines Esau by eternal hatred remains alive to this day, not least in Israel itself, but Genesis permits more than one reading of the relationship between Jacob and Esau. Yes, after Jacob's theft of the inheritance, Esau does hate his brother, but the hatred does not last forever.

When, after 14 years in exile, Jacob returns to the land promised him by his father, he fears a violent confrontation with the brother who has never left the land. Hoping to make amends, Jacob sends ahead lavish gifts, and his generosity seems to succeed. Initially reluctant, Esau finally accepts the gifts and even suggests that the brothers thenceforth journey together. But Jacob declines this offer. He tells Esau to journey on to Seir and promises to join him there later after resting his flocks. After Esau departs, Jacob, unsurprisingly, sets out for Shechem instead.

What Esau proposes is that the two brothers share the land as a single, merged, nomadic clan. What Jacob chooses by his action is a separation of the two clans in two different parts of the land.

Esau's basic willingness to be reconciled with his brother Jacob rests, however, on an earlier, much more dramatic, rarely recognized encounter with him.

The night before the two were to meet, Jacob, fearing for his life, had divided his company and sent both divisions on before him. He, however, remained behind, spending the last night before his anticipated encounter with his brother alone at the Jabbok gorge. There, in the darkness, which he thought to be safe, he was assaulted by an 'iš, a word elsewhere almost always rendered "man." Although this episode is traditionally referred to as Jacob's "wrestling with an angel" (plate 7, p. 83), the text makes no mention of any mal'ak, the usual word for angel in Hebrew. The identity of Jacob's opponent has been inferred from the fact that at the end of their wrestling, Jacob's opponent blesses him: "Your name shall no longer be Jacob, but Israel, for you have striven with God and men [or gods and men] and have prevailed" (Genesis 32:28). Who but God could give such a blessing?

The truth is, of course, that human beings are perfectly capable of blessing one another. Indeed, a human blessing, Isaac's blessing, lay at the heart of the enmity between Jacob and Esau. Jacob had every reason to want Esau to ratify their father's blessing by adding to it a brotherly blessing of his own. The context easily permits us to identify Jacob's attacker as Esau!

Just before dawn, Jacob demands his opponent's name and is told "You must not ask my name," another statement traditionally read as an indication that the nocturnal wrestler is no human being. However, if the visitor was indeed Esau, and if he had been wrestled to a draw by the twin he had thought to best easily, he might well have been loath to speak his own name aloud. This is a story, from beginning to end, of disguises, masquerades, trickery and double meaning. Jacob and Esau were quite literally born wrestling (Genesis 25:26).

Jacob, now renamed Israel by his brother, names the place of his encounter with the 'iš "Penuel, meaning, 'I have seen God face-to-face, and yet my life has been spared,'" (Genesis 32:30). In ways that the reader of Genesis knows and Esau can only guess at, Jacob has indeed striven with God, and irony has ever been one of his weapons. Hours later, when Jacob finally meets Esau face-to-face, Jacob greets his brother with the altogether exceptional statement: "To see your face is like seeing the face of God" (Genesis 33:10). The wordplay in these two verses—on "the face of God ('el)," "the face of God ('elohim)" and "God ('elohim) face-to-face"—is extremely suggestive, especially if we recall that these lines, spoken half-tauntingly to Esau, are also spoken in the hearing of God.

In other words, when Jacob finally meets Esau in broad daylight after 14 years or more of separation, the younger twin (Jacob) tells the elder (Esau) in code that he knows who it was who attacked him by night, that they both know now that the erstwhile mama's boy, the mild and smooth-skinned stay-at-home Jacob (Genesis 25:27, 27:11) has wrestled the hairy hunter, Esau, to a draw, and that Esau is now bound by his own words of blessing as much as by Isaac's.

So then, Esau does not hate Jacob forever. Recall, however, that before the fateful wrestling match, Esau had already had some of the fight taken out of him by lavish and unexpected gifts from his brother. And even after winning, Jacob judges it wiser to divide the land than to merge his clan with his brother's and hold it in common. He has fought his brother to a draw, even a grudging surrender, but it is best not to push for more. After all, father Isaac has blessed Esau too, concluding (did Jacob perhaps know this?):

You shall serve your brother,
But when you grow restive,
You shall break his yoke from your neck.

Genesis 27:40 (JPS)

The blessing referred to in the words immediately following—"And Esau hated Jacob because of the blessing"—would appear to be this blessing rather than Isaac's earlier blessing of Jacob. And its conclusion may be translated either "When you grow restive, you shall break his yoke," or "When you grow restive, break his yoke," a possibility that casts a new light on the line "Esau hated Jacob because of the blessing." The text is provocatively ambiguous. Was Isaac merely predicting or was he in fact licensing and virtually commanding his favorite son to go to war with his twin? Prudence dictated that Jacob not try too hard to find out.

Esau's story does not end at this point. He, too, becomes the father of a nation, the Edomites. His shrine and memorial, in a way, is the Western Wall, the last remnant of the Temple built by that most famous son of Esau, Herod the Idumean, Herod the Edomite, as a place where his brother's offspring and his own could offer sacrifice together to their God.

Reprinted from Bible Review, *October 1998.*

13

THE PATRIARCH JACOB

An "Innocent Man"

CARL D. EVANS

At the beginning of the story of Jacob and Esau, the Bible tells us that Esau was a hunter, a man of the outdoors; Jacob, by contrast, was an *'îš tām* (Genesis 25:27), pronounced *ish tam*. If we were to render this expression in accordance with the Bible's usual meaning of *tām* (*'îš* unquestionably means "man"), we would say that Jacob was a "perfect man," a "blameless man," a "man of integrity" or an "innocent man."

This range of meaning can be gleaned from other biblical passages in which *tām* is used. Job was called an *'îš tām weyāšār*, a "blameless and upright man" (Job 1:1,8, 2:3). Noah was an *'îš ṣaddîq* who was *tāmîm* in his age, a "righteous man ... blameless in his age" (Genesis 6:9). Psalm 37:37 connects *tām* with *yāšār* (the "upright") and the *'îš šālôm* (the "man of integrity").

Clearly '*iš tām* in the biblical idiom usually refers to a man whose character is beyond reproach. And yet, in the case of Jacob, translators have often avoided the plain meaning of '*iš tām*, providing instead ingenious substitutes.

The King James Version says Jacob was a "plain man"; the Revised Standard Version and the Jerusalem Bible say he was a "quiet man"; the new translation of the Jewish Publication Society says a "mild man"; Speiser in the Anchor Bible translates the term as a "retiring man"; the New English Bible says Jacob "led a settled life." The list could go on and on.

Why not an "innocent man" or a "man of integrity" or a "blameless man"? Clearly such a translation has been avoided in many Bibles because the translators are quite aware that, immediately after this characterization, the text tells us how Jacob obtained his elder brother Esau's birthright and later the blessing Isaac intended for Esau. Translators resist the natural meaning of the term '*iš tām* because they perceive Jacob as a deceiving, conniving character.

Lansing Hicks has described the problem quite well:

> The character of Jacob the clever, mendacious supplanter projects so prominently from the narrative that it is difficult to bring the story into proper focus. The reader frequently feels that the deceitful Jacob deserves to be forsaken, left to face alone the full force of his dangers. No other patriarchal narrative is so inescapably dominated by the character of the man himself; and this tends to distort the evaluation of every incident.[1]

How can Jacob be an '*iš tām* in the usual sense of that term if he is also a liar and a cheat?

Traditional Jewish exegetes have interpreted Jacob's character quite differently from their modern counterparts. For example, Rashi, the great Jewish commentator of the 11th century, saw Jacob and Esau as contrasting religious types. Jacob as the '*iš tām* was a man of integrity; his heart and his lips spoke the same language. By contrast, when the Bible in the same verse calls Esau an '*iš* yōdêaʿ ṣayid (literally, "a man who knows hunting"[?]*), it means that Esau knew how to deceive with his mouth. According to Rashi, Esau hypocritically asked his father how tithes were to be taken on salt and straw, to deceive his father into thinking he was very pious.[2] So much for Esau.

Although traditional Jewish exegesis saw Jacob as essentially pure, Hosea the prophet recognizes Jacob as something less than a model of virtue. When Hosea pleads for Israel to return to God, he presents Jacob as someone who, having been punished for his misdeeds, wept and begged for God's favor. The Lord, we are told, was resolved to:

> ... punish Jacob according to his ways,
> And requite him according to his deeds.
>
> Hosea 12:2b

Perhaps these conflicting views of Jacob's character are attributable to the predispositions of the interpreters. Is there a more reliable way of discerning what the biblical author meant when he used the term 'îš tām?

Robert Alter has emphasized the importance of reading biblical narratives from within the imaginative world of the authors of these texts. Alter's studies in literary criticism have shown that the biblical authors' purposeful, artistic use of literary techniques enabled them to depict complexity and moral ambiguity in their characters.[3]

The literary question in this instance is this: Why did the author characterize Jacob as an 'îš tām (an "innocent man") and then place him in a series of concrete situations with other characters that seem to portray Jacob as deceitful and manipulative? Did the narrator want the reader to agree or disagree *with Isaac* that Jacob "came with guile" to take away his brother's blessing (Genesis 27:35)? Did the narrator want us to agree or disagree *with Esau* that Jacob was

---

*Meaning of Hebrew uncertain.

appropriately named because he had supplanted his brother twice, first with the birthright, then with the blessing (Genesis 27:36)?* Did the narrator want us to agree or disagree *with Laban* in charging that his son-in-law Jacob had cheated and stolen from him while amassing a fortune (Genesis 31:26)?

We must distinguish between the author's purview, on the one hand, and the perception of each of the characters, on the other. We must ask what each character knows—or does not know. How does his knowledge color his perception of events? How does his knowledge affect his interpretation of the motivation behind the actions of others? The narrator is, of course, omniscient as he creates the story. How does he disclose to us what he knows, and how does he disclose—or fail to disclose—this to each of the characters?

At the beginning of the Jacob cycle, the author employs a literary device for communicating special knowledge to one of his characters: a divine oracle. The oracle is given to Rebekah, Isaac's wife and Jacob's mother. Rebekah knew that she was pregnant, but was tormented by strange happenings within her womb. Her anguished inquiry of the Lord brings the oracular response: "Two nations are in your womb, and two peoples born of you shall be divided; the one shall be stronger than the other, the elder shall serve the younger" (Genesis 25:23). Thus, Rebekah knows, and the reader knows, that Jacob—not Esau—is to be the child of destiny. But none of the other characters have this knowledge. Rebekah tells no one.

Why doesn't Rebekah tell anyone—not even her husband Isaac? Perhaps the knowledge is too troubling for her to talk about. The right of primogeniture is to be upset and this is certain to cause family strife. Not even Jacob, at least in the beginning, is aware that Providence has decreed that he, not

---

*Jacob, *Ya'aqōbh*, is here derived from the verb *'āqabh*, which is formed from the noun *'āqēbh*, "heel"; thus the verb connotes "to grasp by the heel" or, by extension, "to overreach" or "to supplant."

Esau, shall be the bearer of the divine promise from his generation to the next.

Jacob, then, is initially ignorant of his divinely appointed role.
Thus, when the narrator proceeds to tell us in the next frame that
Jacob is an 'îš tām, he gives us, his readers, a wink. We know that
Jacob is an "innocent man," but the characters in the drama do not.
The reader can only assume that Jacob's innocence will somehow
be demonstrated in the stories that follow.

The opposing nature of the characters of Jacob and of Esau is
reflected in what happens. Esau, the hunter and outdoorsman, comes
in from the field famished. Jacob, the innocent homebody, is mind-
ing his business, cooking a pot of stew. Esau wants Jacob's stew and
says to his brother: "Let me eat some of that red pottage, for I am
famished!" Jacob seizes the opportunity to buy the birthright from
his elder brother, in exchange for the food. The narrator tells us that
Esau "ate and drank, and rose and went his way. Thus Esau despised
his birthright" (Genesis 25:34).

How are we to assess what Jacob has done? Did he take advantage of his brother in a weak moment, acquiring for himself something that was not rightfully his? Or was Jacob innocent?

The narrator supplies the answer. Nothing in the narrative suggests that Jacob did not act within his legal and moral rights. There
is not even a hint of condemnation. We may justifiably conclude
that the narrator did not intend to portray a morally compromised
Jacob. Jacob is innocent of wrongdoing; the guilty party is Esau.
Esau was unworthy of the birthright; he "despised" it or "spurned"
it, the narrator says.

In the next episode, Jacob masquerades as Esau and wins his blind
father's deathbed blessing. It is Rebekah who is responsible for con-
cocting this act of deception. She is the eavesdropper, overhearing the
conversation between Isaac and Esau. Isaac orders his son Esau: "Go
out to the field, and hunt game for me, and prepare for me savory

food, such as I love, and bring it to me that I may eat; that I may bless you before I die" (Genesis 27:3-4). Before Esau can return from the hunt and prepare his father's favorite dish in order to receive his blessing, Rebekah springs into action to deflect the blessing from Esau to Jacob. She acts with dispatch; her instructions are precise. She says to Jacob: "Go to the flock, and fetch me two good kids, that I may prepare from them savory food for your father, such as he loves; and you shall bring it to your father to eat, so that he may bless you before he dies" (Genesis 27:9-10). Her instructions echo Isaac's to Esau. She knows that Isaac's intention runs counter to the realization of the divine oracle. Her knowledge of what Providence has decreed forces her to act. Moreover, she loves Jacob more than Esau.

Jacob is reluctant to go along with the ruse. He objects: "Behold, my brother Esau is a hairy man, and I am a smooth man. Perhaps my father will feel me, and I shall seem to be mocking him, and bring a curse upon myself and not a blessing" (Genesis 27:11-12). But Rebekah insists, claiming that if there is a curse it will fall on her. Jacob fetches the animals, but Rebekah carries out the preparations for the ruse. It is she who makes the savory food; it is she who takes Esau's garments and puts them on Jacob; it is she who thrusts the food into his hand. Once inside Isaac's room, Jacob is left to carry out his mother's act of deception on his own. He says to his father, "I am Esau, your firstborn," and cleverly carries out the ruse.

After Jacob has been blessed, Esau returns from his hunting and the trick is discovered. Isaac says to his disappointed son Esau: "Your brother came with guile, and he has taken away your blessing" (Genesis 27:35). Esau's reply echoes Isaac's low opinion of what Jacob has done: "Is he not rightly named Jacob? For he has supplanted me these two times. He took away my birthright and behold, now he has taken away my blessing" (Genesis 27:36).

But how does the narrator judge what Jacob has done? Does he share Isaac's and Esau's condemnation of Jacob? It is by no means clear that he does. He has gone to great effort to make Rebekah the instigator of the whole affair. Jacob is drawn into the deceptive scheme, but only reluctantly. It is understandable that commentators see Jacob's behavior as a moral lapse, but lest we draw that conclusion too easily, we need to note that the narrator does not make any explicit judgment to that effect. Instead of telling us how to judge Jacob's behavior, the narrator chooses to let us ponder as we read on.

Rebekah's craftiness is further evidenced in the next episode, where she is again a manipulator of events. On hearing that Esau is so angry that he is determined to kill Jacob, Rebekah warns Jacob and instructs him to flee at once to her brother Laban in Haran. Her opening words are a precise echo of the previous episode when she enlisted Jacob's participation in tricking Isaac (Genesis 27:8). Again she says to Jacob, "Now, my son, listen to me" (Genesis 27:43). She will trick Isaac again. She tells Jacob one thing, and she will tell Isaac another. Jacob must go to stay with Laban, Isaac is told, because it is time for Jacob to take a wife.[4] She communicates the urgency of the situation by stating, "I am weary of my life because of the Hittite women. If Jacob marries one of the Hittite women such as these, one of the women of the land, what good will my life be to me?" (Genesis 27:46).

Isaac, unaware that he has again been deceived by his wife, obligingly responds to her frantic plea. He summons Jacob, instructs him to go to the ancestral homeland to marry one of Laban's daughters, blesses him in the name of El Shaddai and sends him on his way. Rebekah has cleverly manipulated her husband a second time, and Jacob is blessed again before his departure.

With this blessing, pronounced by his father Isaac, Jacob learns for the first time that the Almighty has conferred on him the blessing of Abraham, to be passed on by Jacob to his own descendants.

> May El Shaddai bless you, make you fertile and numerous, so that you become an assembly of peoples. May He grant the blessing of Abraham to you and your offspring, that you may possess the land where you are sojourning, which God gave to Abraham.
>
> Genesis 28:3-4

Through her carefully crafted schemes, Rebekah has been a mid-wife to Providence. Jacob now knows his special place in the chain of generations.

In the next episode, this judgment is confirmed by God himself in the dream of the ladder extending to heaven with angels going up and down. The Lord says to Jacob as he sleeps with his head upon a stone:

> I am the Lord, the God of your father Abraham and the God of Isaac: the ground on which you are lying I will give to you and to your offspring. Your descendants shall be as the dust of the earth; you shall spread out to the west and to the east, to the north and to the south. All the families of the earth shall bless themselves by you and your descendants.
>
> Genesis 28:13-14

We shall not follow Jacob to Laban's house and back, except to note, as many commentators have observed, that the stories of Jacob's experiences in Haran contain numerous subtle connections with the stories we have just reviewed—for example, Laban's deception of Jacob by substituting Leah for Rachel, followed by Laban's explanation: "It is not so done in our country to give the younger before the firstborn" (Genesis 29:26). But does this story, rich in associations with Jacob's acquisition of the firstborn's blessing from his blind father, imply a moral judgment of Jacob? Has the author created the subtle connections in order to show that the perpetrator of deception has now become the victim? Is the narrator passing an adverse moral judgment on Jacob's earlier actions?

Admittedly, the story can be read in that way. But another interpretation is at least equally plausible. Jacob, again, has been drawn into a plot against his will. For seven years Laban led him on, and Jacob innocently participated in the scheme. He did not know Laban's mind, and he fell victim to his sinister workings. The narrator wants us to note, however, that Jacob did not let his unfortunate plight do him in. He dutifully agreed—without complaint or a word of resentment—to work seven more years for Rachel. Unfortunately, the result was that Jacob was drawn into still another round of strife, set up by the rivalry between Leah and Rachel, another story of older and younger siblings.

From beginning to end, the stories about Jacob can be read as the narrator's imaginative effort to maintain Jacob's innocence—to be consistent with his opening characterization of Jacob as an 'îš tām. To this end, the storyteller puts Jacob, time and again, into situations of strife and conflict that test the patriarch's character. When Jacob is not yet aware of his divinely appointed destiny as the supplanter of Esau, he strives innocently to obtain Esau's birthright; having obtained it by legitimate means, he then resists his mother's deceitful plan to win the blessing Isaac intends for Esau. When Rebekah insists, Jacob becomes a reluctant, but effective, participant in the scheme. And yet it is he—not his mother—who receives the harsh judgments of his father and brother. In Haran, it is Laban who conspires to take advantage of Jacob, and yet Laban will later accuse Jacob, wrongly, of cheating and theft. And so it goes. Despite his difficulties, and despite repeated assaults on his character, Jacob remains an "innocent man," an 'îš tām.

The narrator deliberately withholds his explicit judgment of Jacob—except to describe him at the outset as an 'îš tām. And the description is delightfully ambiguous! While Jacob is kept in the dark about his appointed destiny (thus preserving his *cognitive* innocence), the narrator allows his characters, who likewise are unaware of the divine plan, to condemn the patriarch time and again. Thus, the question of Jacob's *moral* innocence hovers disturbingly over each successive episode.[5] In the end, however, the narrator's verdict on the patriarch—did he do right? did he do wrong?—is announced in the words of the mysterious one with whom Jacob struggled at the Jabbok (Penuel) on his journey back to Canaan from Haran. Here the narrator at long last articulates the meaning of

Jacob's struggles: "Your name shall no more be called Jacob, but
Israel, for you have striven with God and with men, and have pre-
vailed" (Genesis 32:28). Indeed, Jacob had!
Reprinted from Bible Review, *Spring 1986.*

[1]Lansing Hicks, "Jacob (Israel)," *Interpreter's Dictionary of the Bible*, Vol. 2 (Nashville, TN:
Abingdon, 1962), pp. 782-787, esp. 784.

[2]*Pentateuch with Targum Onkelos, Haphtaroth and Prayers for Sabbath and Rashi's Commentary,*
trans. M. Rosenbaum and Dr. A.M. Silbermann (London: Shapire, Vallentine & Co., 1946);
"Genesis," esp. p. 116.

[3]Robert Alter, *The Art of Biblical Narrative* (New York: Basic Books, 1981). Alter shows
how the biblical narrators introduce playful and subtle articulations of the human situation. Although his reading of the Jacob stories is very sensitive and enlightening (and I
approve his technique), I, nevertheless, do not believe he resolves the problems of
Jacob's "innocence."

Alter notes that *tām* is an "odd epithet" when attached to Jacob and thus contains "a
lurking possibility of irony" (p. 183). But he leaves the suggestion barren. The use of this
particular epithet immediately before Jacob's acquisition of Esau's birthright "is bound to
give us pause," he admits, "to make us puzzle over the moral nature of Jacob—an enigma
we shall be trying to fathom twenty chapters later" (p. 43ff.).

[4]Source critics often attribute Genesis 27:46-28:9 to P, the Priestly writer, rather than to the
author of the rest of the cycle. I take the story here, however, in its final redacted form.

[5]Compare Job 9:20-22 where the moral and cognitive connotations of *tām* alternate in
the poignant complaint of Job, who, like Jacob, is left in the dark about the meaning of
his struggle.

14

DECEPTION FOR DECEPTION

Who Breaks the Cycle?

RICHARD ELLIOTT FRIEDMAN

The biblical story of Jacob is artistically an exquisite creation, psychologically an intriguing portrait and religiously an interpretive treasure-house—but it has always been a problem. Even Sunday school children ask why the hero Jacob, the great patriarch, withholds food from his own brother Esau to get his brother's birthright and then lies to his blind father Isaac on Isaac's deathbed to get his father to give him his brother's blessing. Why did the ancient Israelite author tell the story this way, portraying his own ancestor as manipulative of and deceitful to his family?

Moreover, it is not Jacob alone who is portrayed as a deceiver. His mother Rebekah, his uncle Laban, his wife Rachel and most of his sons become involved in deception as well. Why conceive of such a story? Why include it in sacred literature?

Stories of complex and infectious intrafamily conflict have long—perhaps always—been the subject of powerful literature. A comedian used to tell the story of *Hamlet*: At the end, Ophelia has drowned, her father Polonius has been run through with a sword, her brother Laertes and her lover Hamlet lie dead onstage from poisoned swords, Hamlet's mother Gertrude lies dead of a poisoned drink, Hamlet's uncle Claudius lies dead from Hamlet's thrust of Laertes' sword. The comedian suggested the ghost of Hamlet's father, who opened the play, should then walk onto the stage and say to the audience with a sigh, "You see? Go try and raise a family."

Hamlet is only one example in a group of portrayals of family conflict that includes the families of Agamemnon and Karamazov. In our Freudian age, it hardly seems necessary to explain why this subject matter is so rich artistically and so powerful dramatically. It should hardly surprise us, therefore, that such a story appears in the Bible.

The story of Jacob is the story of a family. The family is split geographically. Half lives in Canaan, half in Mesopotamia. The Bible focuses on the branch in Canaan, but because of the conflict within the family, the story moves to Mesopotamia when Jacob goes there; then shifts, after 20 years, back to Canaan; and finally culminates, in Joseph's time, in Egypt.

From the very beginning, the story of Jacob is about conflict. Jacob and his twin brother Esau fight in their mother Rebekah's womb. Esau is born first, but Jacob reaches out from the womb to hold him back. Because Esau's birth priority is given as a fact, Jacob's conflict with his brother requires him to find some means of circumventing that fact. The means is *deception*.

The story soon becomes an account of a family whose members are constantly deceiving one another. Jacob, with Rebekah's help, deceives Esau and Isaac to get for himself the birthright and blessing. Jacob's uncle Laban deceives Jacob by substituting Laban's elder daughter Leah for the younger daughter Rachel, whom Jacob loves.

Jacob, in turn, deceives Laban over ownership of their livestock. Rachel deceives her father Laban over possession of the family's icons. Jacob's own sons then deceive him concerning the disappearance of their brother Joseph. Joseph deceives his brothers concerning the fate that awaits them in Egypt. Jacob's sons Simeon and Levi deceive the people of Shechem over an injury to their sister Dinah. Jacob's son Judah deceives his own daughter-in-law Tamar by reneging on his promise to let her marry his last son. Tamar, in turn, deceives Judah to expose his wrongful deception. Go try and raise a family.

The theme of deception as reflected in these stories has not gone unnoticed. Literary and theological interpreters of Genesis have commented on it for centuries—and they are troubled by it. What are we to think of Jacob's behavior—and of Rebekah's and Rachel's and Judah's? Some interpreters try to vindicate Jacob, to rationalize his actions, to disparage Esau or to come to terms in other ways with what Jacob does. But how does the biblical text itself treat this matter? How does the biblical author present the story of these acts and their consequences? The fact is that for every act of deception, an ironic recompense occurs later in the story. The consistency of this recompense indicates that the biblical author is specifically developing the theme of deception and its recompense to a denouement at the end of the story.

Jacob's first action is to obtain his brother Esau's birthright, which will entitle Jacob to a double portion of their father Isaac's property after his death. The story is well known: Esau returns from hunting, famished, and asks his brother for food; Jacob insists that Esau sell him his birthright in return for some lentil stew. Esau says that the birthright will do him no good if he dies of hunger, and he capitulates and sells Jacob his birthright. Jacob then gives him bread and stew (Genesis 25:29-34).

Jacob's recompense comes years later in an equally famous story. Jacob loves his cousin Rachel, and he agrees to work for her father Laban for seven years for Rachel's hand in marriage.

But at the end of the seven years, on the morning after the wedding night, Jacob finds that Laban has substituted Rachel's older sister, Leah, for Rachel. Jacob asks his uncle/father-in-law, "Why have you deceived me?" Laban answers: "It is not done thus in our place, to give the younger before the *firstborn*" (Genesis 29:26).[1] Not "the younger before the *elder*," but "the younger before the *firstborn*."* The man who took away the firstborn privilege of his brother has now suffered because of the firstborn privilege of his beloved's sister.

Is this reference to Leah as the firstborn a chance detail based on a coincidence of language, or is it an essential development in the structure of the story?

Jacob's second action is to get the blessing that his father Isaac intends for Esau, a blessing of both prosperity and dominion. Isaac, now old and blind, not knowing when he will die, asks Esau to hunt some game and prepare a meal for him, after which he will bless Esau. Isaac's wife Rebekah loves Jacob, however. She tells Jacob that she has overheard what Isaac told Esau. She sends Jacob to the flocks to bring back two choice goat kids, and from this she prepares a meal for Isaac like the meal Isaac has asked Esau to prepare. She then sends her preferred son Jacob to pose as Esau to his blind father and thus to gain the birthright: To deceive his father, Jacob wears Esau's clothing, which bears the smell of the hunter brother. The skins of kids cover Jacob's arms to imitate his brother's hairy skin. Thus attired, Jacob brings Isaac the meal Rebekah has prepared. Isaac asks who has come to him. Jacob replies, "I am Esau, your firstborn." Isaac draws Jacob to him and feels his hairy skin: "The voice is the voice of Jacob, but the hands are the hands of Esau," he says. Then Isaac eats the meal and draws Jacob to him once again. Isaac smells the clothes Jacob is

*The Aramaic translation (the Targum), the Greek translation (the Septuagint), and, recently, the New English Bible and the New Jewish Publication Society translations all make it "the older," not "the firstborn," thus unfortunately missing this point and making it unavailable to their readers.

wearing—Esau's clothes. Jacob kisses his father, who then blesses him with the blessing meant for Esau.

When the deception becomes known, Isaac trembles, and Esau weeps in bitter anguish, "Bless me too, father." Isaac answers: "Your brother came with deception and took away your blessing." Esau cries out, "Isn't his name Jacob [*to catch*]! He's caught me these two times! He took away my birthright and now he has taken away my blessing" (Genesis 27:34-36).

Years later, Jacob is paid back for this, too. His own sons, jealous of Jacob's preferred son Joseph, sell Joseph into slavery in Egypt. They dip Joseph's coat of many colors in the blood of a goat and take it to the now elderly Jacob. "We found this," the brothers say, as they display it before their father. "Recognize this!" they tell Jacob. Jacob *recognized* it, the text notes: "It is my son's coat; a wild animal has eaten him" (Genesis 37:33). Jacob rends his clothes and wears sackcloth in mourning for his son (plate 9, p. 85). His other children seek to comfort him, but he refuses to be comforted. "Thus his father bewailed [Joseph]." And thus was Jacob deceived.

More particularly, Jacob once deceived *his* father with his *brother's clothing* and the meat and hide of a *goat*. Now his sons deceive with their *brother's clothing* and the blood of a *goat*. Worse, Jacob really deceives *himself* in response to his sons' request that he "recognize" the coat. Worse still, the word that is used for "goat" in the Joseph story is *sēʿîr;* Seʿir is the name of the place where *Esau* settles (Genesis 33:16). We are thus subtly reminded of the connection between the two stories.*

I have already recounted how Laban deceives Jacob by substituting Leah for Rachel. Laban, too, is repaid in the same coin when, years later, Jacob deceives him back. In return for his continued work for Laban, Jacob asks for all the spotted, striped and brown sheep and goats among Laban's flocks. Laban agrees. Jacob, who is in

*The pun is actually a double one; Esau is described as a "hairy man," which was the reason for the goatskin deception in the first place, and "hairy" in Hebrew is *śāʿîr* (Genesis 27:11).

charge of the flocks, then connives (by magic? miracle? paragenetics?) to produce such colored sheep and goats in great numbers, until he is rich in ewes and rams (Genesis 30:28-43). Thus Jacob deceives Laban back. Laban has deceived him over *Rachel* and *Leah*; Jacob has paid Laban back by getting his ewes and rams.

In Hebrew, ewes and rams are *r^eḥēlîm* and *'êlîm* (Genesis 32:14, 31:38). That is, Rachel (*rāḥēl*) in Hebrew means "ewe," and the word for "ram" (*'ayil*) is a twist of the name of Leah. Because Laban deceived Jacob by substituting Leah for Rachel, Laban is now repaid by losing his ewes and his rams (his Rachels and Leahs). Here, again, the payback contains a hint of the original offense.

Like father, like daughter: Next Rachel deceives her father Laban. Perhaps this, too, is in further recompense for his having substituted Leah for her at the wedding. But Rachel, too, is paid back, as we shall see. The time comes when Jacob leaves Laban's house. He departs secretly with his wives and children, his flocks and his belongings. Unknown to Jacob, his beloved Rachel steals her father's household icons, the *teraphim*. Three days later Laban discovers that Jacob and his family have fled and that his icons are missing. Laban pursues Jacob and catches up with him. Laban charges Jacob with having stolen his *teraphim*. Jacob, not knowing that Rachel has stolen the icons, allows Laban to search the camp and tells him, "With whomever you find your gods, let that person not live" (Genesis 31:32). Laban searches all the tents for his *teraphim*. When he comes to Rachel's tent, she hides the idols in her camel saddle and sits on it (plate 8, p. 84). She tells her father: "I cannot get up before you because the way of women is with me" (Genesis 31:35).

Thus Rachel deceives her father and successfully appropriates his *teraphim*, perhaps in recompense for his having denied her her wedding night with the husband who had labored for her for seven years.

But Rachel's deception proves to be the costliest of all. Jacob, not knowing that she has stolen the icons, has unwittingly cursed his wife: "With whomever you find your gods, let that person not live."

Rachel has deceived her father by claiming to be menstruating. Four chapters later Rachel dies in childbirth—which involves the cessation of menstruation.

Like father, like sons: We have already seen how Jacob's sons deceive their father over their sale of Joseph into Egyptian slavery; they take Joseph's coat of many colors, dip it in a goat's blood and take it back to their father Jacob to deceive him into believing that Joseph, the first son of the beloved Rachel, has been devoured by wild beasts.

Years later, when Joseph has risen to extraordinary power in Egypt, he, in turn, deceives his brothers. Jacob sends the brothers to Egypt to buy food, for the famine in Canaan is severe; in Egypt the stores are bulging, thanks to Joseph's wise administration, to say nothing of his ability to foresee the seven-year drought.

When the brothers arrive in Egypt, Joseph interrogates them, but they do not recognize Joseph, now the chief dispenser of rations of grain. Repeatedly they refer to themselves as "your slaves" as they speak to Joseph, whom they once sold as a slave (Genesis 42:10-13, 44:9,16,21,23,31). Again, the deception for deception theme is developed subtly in the text.

The ten brothers (excluding Benjamin) had sold Joseph into slavery for 20 measures of silver. When they come to Egypt to buy grain, they are repaid with 20 measures of silver. The story is a bit complicated, but the point is clear. Joseph first accuses the brothers of being spies from Canaan. They, of course, deny it. They are, they say, ten of 12 sons of a man from the land of Canaan, one son having died (Joseph) and the other (the youngest, Benjamin) having remained home with his father. Supposedly to test whether they are telling the truth, Joseph keeps Simeon and sends the other nine back to Canaan to return with Benjamin. To confuse them further, Joseph secretly has each measure of silver that they have paid for the grain placed back in the sacks of the nine brothers. Later, they return with their youngest brother, Benjamin, to buy more food. Joseph releases Simeon and sends off all 11 brothers, but again, he secretly has their silver placed back in their sacks, this time of 11 brothers. Thus Joseph has returned a total of 20 measures of silver—the same as the price for which the brothers sold Joseph into slavery (Genesis 37:28, 42:3-25, 43:15-44:1). The brothers thus receive 20 measures of silver a second time, but this time under very different circumstances. They learn what it means to feel helpless, to be the victims of injustice. And, as they deceived, they are deceived.

Reuben, the oldest brother, had originally opposed selling Joseph and indeed had not been present at the time of the deed. It was, therefore, *Simeon*, the second oldest, who was responsible—and it was he who imprisoned to assure the return of the brothers with Benjamin. Thus Simeon, too, apparently received a hidden recompense for his role in the sale and deception.

The deception—and its recompense—continues. Jacob's son Judah deceives his daughter-in-law Tamar. Judah has three sons. Judah marries his oldest son to Tamar. But the son soon dies without children. The second son then marries Tamar to provide offspring for the deceased brother, but the second son also dies. Although Judah promises Tamar that he will give her his third son, Shelah, he is fearful that Shelah, too, may die if he marries Tamar. Judah therefore deceives Tamar by telling her that Shelah is still too young for marriage and that she should wait a while. She has a long wait. Shelah grows up, but Judah makes no wedding plans. Tamar poses as a veiled prostitute on the road. Judah, now a widower, sees her and is attracted to her. He sleeps with her, and he promises to pay her one goat. As a pledge for the payment, he leaves an article of his clothing, among other things. When Judah sends to redeem his pledge, Tamar is nowhere to be found. Some time later, Judah learns that his daughter-in-law is pregnant. Since Tamar is still officially bound to Judah's son Shelah, this is the equivalent of adultery. Judah says that Tamar should be burned for this offense, but Tamar produces Judah's pledge items and says, "Recognize these."

He does—and acknowledges that he has wronged her. Like father, like son. The deceiver has been deceived. Judah deceived Tamar; Tamar has deceived him. And the retribution fits the original deception. He denies her a man; she makes him her man. Moreover, this deception involves clothing (the pledge) and a goat (the payment)—just as Jacob deceived his father Isaac by donning his brother's clothing and giving him the cooked meal of a goat and just as the brothers deceived Jacob concerning Joseph—with Joseph's coat dipped in the blood of a goat. Moreover, the story of Judah and Tamar culminates with "recognize" (the pledge items Judah had given her), just as Jacob was told to "recognize" the clothing (the coat of many colors) dipped in the blood of a goat. Thus clothing and a goat are thrice involved in deceptions.

Tamar gives birth to *twins*. Like Jacob and Esau, they struggle to be first out of the womb! Because they are Judah's sons, not Shelah's, they are replacements for Judah's two sons who died after marrying Tamar (Genesis 38).

Three other sons of Jacob commit acts of costly deception. Jacob's firstborn son Reuben deceives his father by sleeping with Jacob's concubine Bilhah, but Jacob finds out (Genesis 35:22).

Jacob's second- and third-born sons, Simeon and Levi, deceive the people of the city of Shechem. The prince of that city, whose name is also Shechem, has slept with their sister Dinah and only later asked for her hand in marriage. Her brothers respond to the proposal with deception, saying that they will only permit intermarriage with the Shechemites if the latter circumcise all their males. The Shechemites agree to the surgery, and when the Shechemite men are immobile from the pain of the circumcisions, Simeon and Levi come and massacre the city. Jacob criticizes them for this act, but they answer, "Shall he treat our sister like a prostitute?" (Genesis 34).

The price that Reuben, Simeon and Levi pay for their deceptions is loss of place in the succession to the birthright. On his deathbed (plate 10, page 86), Jacob explicitly takes away Reuben's preeminence because he has slept with Bilhah ("When you mounted your father's bed you brought disgrace" [Genesis 49:3-4]) and condemns Simeon and Levi to dispersal ("When angry they slay men" [Genesis 49:5-7]). The honor goes to the fourth son, Judah ("The sceptre shall not depart from Judah" [Genesis 49:8-10]).

Every deception is paid back. All of the deceivers are deceived.

What started this chain of deceptions? What brings it to an end?

It is difficult to say what started it. Perhaps, from the biblical authors' point of view, it was a matter of destiny, a complex series of twists of events that explained how the people of Israel came to be residing in Egypt. Or perhaps we should look for the root and model of this family's inclination for deception prior to Jacob. After all, Jacob's father Isaac tried to deceive the Philistine king Abimelech into believing Isaac's wife Rebekah was his sister (Genesis 26). Isaac's father Abraham had tried the same deception on the same king and on the Egyptian king as well (Genesis 20 and 12). Does the chain of deceptions begin with Rebekah, who helps her preferred son Jacob to deceive Isaac? Or does it begin with Isaac? Or with Abraham? Or perhaps with the snake in the Garden of Eden?

It is easier to identify what brings this chain of deception to an end: forgiveness. The sequence of deceptions that causes this family so much suffering finally comes to an end when Joseph chooses not to take revenge on his brothers. True, Joseph causes them discomfort, but only to the point of their recognizing their past wrong. He does them no harm corresponding to what they have done to him, despite the fact that it is clearly in his power to do so. So much of the Book of Genesis is about this family's deceptions, but the book's last chapter is a touching portrayal of forgiveness. After Jacob dies, the brothers say to one another, "He [Joseph] will certainly pay us back all the harm that we did him."

But they soon learn that their younger brother is no longer the simple teenager who once naively offended them by telling them his grandiose dreams. He rejects deception and retaliation.

And Joseph said to them, "Do not be afraid, for am I in the place of God? You intended harm for me. God intended it for good: in order to do as it is today, to keep a large people alive. And now do not be afraid. I shall provide for you and your children." And he comforted them, and he spoke on their hearts.

Genesis 50:15-21

Wherever the deception begins, it ends when one family member puts family above revenge, when one who is manifestly entitled to retribution chooses not to take it.

Joseph changes from what one could describe as a thoughtless teenager to a sensitive, powerful man. No equivalent character development is to be found in Adam, Noah, Abraham, Sarah, Isaac or Rebekah. They all remain basically constant figures through the stories about them.

The one other figure who undergoes dramatic character development equal to Joseph's is Jacob. Here the matter of deception is intimately related to his character development. As Esau points out, Jacob's very name connotes deception: to catch. Jacob's name also recalls his earliest conflict with Esau because the name Jacob is related to the Hebrew word for heel ($\bar{A}q\bar{e}b$). The Bible itself tells us Jacob is given this name because he reached out from the womb to try to grab his twin Esau's heel—ostensibly to pull him back and be the firstborn (Genesis 25:26). But Jacob changes after his experiences in Mesopotamia. He has been the deceiver and the deceived. He has hurt and been hurt. He is now a husband and a father, a man who has struggled and prospered. For the rest of the story he is no longer portrayed as a man of action but, more often, as a relatively passive man, seeking to appease his brother, avoiding strife and risk. And precisely at the juncture that marks this change in Jacob's character, he has his encounter with God (or an angel?) at Penuel (plate 7, p. 83). As Jacob is about to re-enter the land of Canaan after the long journey from Laban's house, he wrestles alone with this extraordinary being until the break of day. Jacob will not let him go until he blesses Jacob. "What is your name?" he asks Jacob. When Jacob tells him, he replies, "Your name shall no longer be Jacob, but Israel (*Yiśrā-'ēl*), for you have struggled with Elohim [God] and men, and prevailed." In this verse the name Israel is understood to mean "the one who has struggled with God." The Hebrew word for struggled (*ś-r-h*) is related to the first two syllables in the Hebrew word for Israel (*Yiśrā-'ēl*).

Is this divine encounter the signpost of the change in Jacob's character, or the cause? Either way, as his character changes and he ceases to be the deceiver, just then he sheds the name Jacob (the one who catches) and becomes instead Israel (the one who has struggled with God) (Genesis 32:25-29).

The Bible does not "clean up" Jacob the way some Sunday schools, *midrashim* and modern interpreters do. The biblical writers seem to have been quite content to leave their heroes imperfect.

Why? Why should the author even conceive of such a story? Perhaps he saw deception in the world around him or, for that matter, in his own family, and wanted to say, "It comes back." Perhaps he meant this as a message to his people? To his wife? To his children? To his in-laws?

Or perhaps he conceived it in literary protest against the ancient Near Eastern practice of glorifying national heroes. As has been frequently observed, to read the ancient reports, one would think that no Near Eastern king ever lost a battle. In this respect, it is tantalizing to compare the Jacob cycle to the Court History of David in 2 Samuel. The similarity in style, concerns and actual portrayals of events between these two works is so striking that scholars have occasionally suggested that they are by the same author. Not the least among the similarities is that the Court History, too, manifestly develops the idea of deception for deception. For example, after King David sleeps with Uriah's wife Bathsheba and she becomes pregnant, David schemes to deceive Uriah into thinking Uriah himself is the father of the child in his wife's womb. When this fails, David plots successfully to have the devoted Uriah killed in battle. The prophet Nathan then deceives King David by concealing the underlying message of a story he tells David about a rich man with a great flock who steals from a poor friend with but one lamb in order to get food to entertain a guest. David flies into a rage at Nathan's story and proclaims that the rich man deserves to die. "And Nathan said to David, 'That man is you!'" (2 Samuel 12:1-7). Nathan thus exposes David's crime with a deceptive story, causing David to condemn himself.

But David pays a price for his deception of Uriah. The price involves a series of deceptions among his children. Here again a Judean author was prepared to describe the founder of the national dynasty critically.

For whatever purpose the author of the Jacob cycle conceived this story, the fact is that he, among other biblical writers, had a realistic impulse, a sense of the true psychological complexity of families: sibling rivalry, fathers and sons in conflict, mothers finding channels of influence in male family structures, women torn between fathers and husbands. Would a story of idealized heroes have been more effective, more inspiring?

There is another value to this kind of treatment—a theological value. By not glorifying its human heroes, the text glorifies its other central figure, the deity. The message here, repeated through the generations described in the Hebrew Bible, apparently is that God can work through anyone: through a deceiver, a straying king or a man, who, like Moses, has a "heavy mouth and heavy tongue" (Exodus 4:10). A prophet can be a layperson (Isaiah 6:5), a priest (Jeremiah 1:1) or a cowherd (Amos 7:14).

The principles of divine selection are usually inscrutable. God gives Rebekah an oracle while she is still carrying the twins Jacob and Esau in her womb; the oracle tells her that her younger son will dominate the elder. Does the oracle reflect divine *foreknowledge* or divine *control*? When she attempts to influence the outcome herself, is she acting in pious obedience to the oracle? Or is she acting out of loyalty to her preferred son? As usual, the Bible's literary and theological ambiguities are as interesting as its articulated facts.

The deception-for-deception sequence is not obvious in the narrative. The writer did not hit his readers over the head with it. He developed his point through a story, not by a pronouncement. And he wove it through the story, so that generations of readers would have the burden of seeking it out—and the pleasure of discovering it.

And so it is that the Bible has had, concealed within it, treasures of art and ideas, some intended by the authors and some not, for successive generations to uncover. Splendid puns lie embedded in the Book of Jonah for millennia, and gradually they are identified, until the work is recognized as an elaborate fabric of wordplay.[2] The Song of Deborah (Judges 5) is identified, after millennia, as the poetic source of the prose history of Deborah in Judges 4.[3] New generations come with new methods, new interests and new sensitivities. This chapter is an example of the literary study of the Bible being used by the present generation of biblical scholars. Literary study, enriched with historical, theological and psychological study, is playing its part in bringing to light more of the Bible's concealed treasures. The Bible at its richest has not yet been read.

Reprinted from Bible Review, *Spring 1986.*

[1]Genesis 29:26. Several scholars have discussed this irony in various terms: Ephraim A. Speiser, *Genesis*, Anchor Bible 1 (Garden City, NY: Doubleday, 1964), p. 227; Nahum Sarna, *Understanding Genesis* (New York: Schocken, 1966), p. 184; Michael Fishbane, *Text and Texture* (New York: Schocken, 1979), p. 55ff.; Robert Alter (citing Umberto Cassuto), "Sacred History and Prose Fiction," in *The Creation of Sacred Literature*, ed. Richard E. Friedman (Berkeley: Univ. of California Press, 1981), p. 23. Fishbane's discussion of recompense for deception is especially interesting in parallel with what follows here.

[2]Friedman and Baruch Halpern, "Composition and Paronomasia in the Book of Jonah," *Hebrew Annual Review* 4 (1980), pp. 79-92.

[3]Halpern, "The Uneasy Compromise Between the Israelite Source and the Biblical Historian," in *The Poet and the Historian: Essays in Literary and Historical Biblical Criticism*, Harvard Semitic Studies, ed. Friedman (Chico, CA: Scholars Press, 1983), pp. 46-99.

15

JACOB'S TERRIBLE BURDEN

In the Shadow of the Text

GORDON TUCKER

There is scarcely a more poignant human story of love and tragedy in the Bible—if not in all of literature—than that of the patriarch Jacob and his beloved Rachel. Sent to Haran by his father, Isaac, to find a wife among the daughters of his mother's brother Laban, Jacob meets Laban's daughter Rachel as she comes to water her flocks. Jacob instantly falls in love with the beautiful Rachel and offers to work for his uncle Laban for seven years to earn the right to marry his younger daughter. Laban agrees and "Jacob served seven years for Rachel, and they seemed to him but a few days because of his love for her" (Genesis 29:20). The night of the wedding feast, Laban secretly substitutes his older daughter Leah for her sister Rachel. The unsuspecting Jacob consummates the marriage with Leah, thinking she is Rachel, for whom he has yearned these seven years.

But "when morning came, there was Leah!" (Genesis 29:25). Jacob is enraged. The deceitful Laban explains: "It is not the practice in our place to marry off the younger before the older. Wait until the bridal week of [Leah] is over and we will give you [Rachel] too, provided you serve me another seven years" (Genesis 29:27). Defeated, Jacob waits the week, then cohabits with Rachel. "And [Jacob] served [Laban] for another seven years" (Genesis 29:30).

In the years after the marriage, both Leah and Rachel (as well as each of their maidservants) bear children to Jacob. Leah's children— six sons and a daughter—come rapidly, one after the other, while Rachel, barren, despairs of ever conceiving. Finally, "God remembered Rachel ... and opened her womb" (Genesis 30:22). She names her firstborn "Joseph, meaning, in Hebrew, 'May the Lord add (yosef) another son for me'" (Genesis 30:24).

After 20 years, Jacob decides to return to Canaan. He takes his wives and children and leaves Laban to return to the land of his father Isaac. Rachel again becomes pregnant, and on the journey she dies in childbirth. Her second son, however, survives the birth and is named "Benjamin" by Jacob. The grieving Jacob buries Rachel, not in the ancestral burial ground at the Cave of Machpelah, which Abraham purchased in Hebron from Ephron the Hittite, but on the road to Ephrath near Bethlehem.

For millennia, Rachel's roadside tomb has symbolized what it means to be exiled—not at rest, not at peace. It may be, however, that not only Rachel herself, but an important part of her story as well, was left at the side of the road. What follows is an effort to reclaim that story, buried deep in Scripture.

A number of puzzling things about Jacob are reported in Genesis. They are all resolved when we recognize two heart-rending facts: One, which emerges from a close, careful reading of the text, is that an oath made by Jacob was responsible for Rachel's death—and that he came to know it. The other fact is more dimly present but also significant:

that Jacob believed that by this oath he may have unwittingly doomed both Joseph and Benjamin. Together, let us unravel the ancient tale.

The Dutch scholar Jan P. Fokkelman calls Jacob a "conjurer with stones."[1] Three times in Jacob's life, stones play important roles. Jacob, as a young man on his way to find a wife in Haran,* stops at Bethel for the night and rests his head on a stone (Genesis 28:11). There Jacob dreams of a stairway reaching to the sky with angels going up and down, and there God appears, promising Jacob "the ground on which you are lying ... Your descendants shall be as the dust of the earth ... All the families of the earth shall bless themselves by you and your descendants ... I will protect you wherever you go and will bring you back to this land" (Genesis 28:13-15).

Completing his journey to Laban in Haran, Jacob comes to a well where he sees Rachel, the daughter of his uncle Laban, tending her father's flock. Jacob "rolled the stone off the mouth of the well, and watered the flock" (Genesis 29:10). Once again, a stone marks a critical moment for Jacob.

The third incident marked by stones occurs 20 years later, when Jacob parts from his father-in-law Laban and they make a pact. Jacob "took stones and made a mound," which Laban names Yegar-sahadutha but Jacob calls Gal-Ed (Aramaic and Hebrew respectively for "mound of witness") (Genesis 31:46-47). Laban declares the mound to be "'a witness between you and me this day ... If you ill-treat my daughters or take other wives besides my daughters ... God himself will be witness between you and me. I am not to cross to you past this mound, and ... you are not to cross to me ... with hostile intent.' ... And Jacob swore by the Fear of his father Isaac" (Genesis 31:47-53).

The stones on these three occasions are surely significant, but no great puzzle. But on four other occasions, Jacob also erects a *matzevah* (plural, *matzevot*), an upright stone with an apparently cultic function. Those four incidents actually occur in only three locations, since

---

*Jacob is also fleeing from his jealous brother Esau, who seeks to kill him because Jacob stole the blessing meant for him (Genesis 27:41-44).

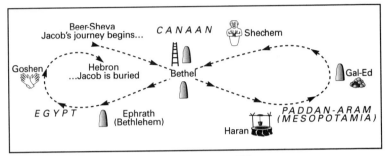

JACOB'S JOURNEY

Beer-Sheva: Jacob leaves Canaan.

Bethel: Jacob dreams of a ladder to heaven and sets up a standing stone, or matzevah.

Haran: Jacob meets Laban's daughter Rachel at a well. Twenty years later, Jacob leaves Haran with his wives and children. Rachel steals Laban's household idols, or teraphim.

Gal-Ed: Jacob erects a matzevah and a stone mound to mark his non-hostility pact with Laban. Unaware of Rachel's theft of her father's teraphim, Jacob vows death to anyone with whom Laban's household gods are found.

Shechem: While burying the teraphim outside Bethel, Jacob must have realized that Rachel had stolen them.

Bethel: God appears again to Jacob, blesses him and changes his name to Israel. Jacob erects another matzevah.

Ephrath (Bethlehem): Rachel dies; Jacob marks her grave with a matzevah.

Goshen: Jacob adopts Joseph's sons Ephraim and Manasseh and blesses them.

Hebron: Joseph buries Jacob at the Cave of Machpelah.

one is the site of two *matzevot* (see map, above). The first takes place at Bethel where Jacob has his dream of a ladder and where, as we have seen, he rests his head on a stone. Upon awakening, Jacob "took the stone that he had put under his head and set it up as a pillar (*matzevah*) and poured oil on the top of it" (Genesis 28:18).[2]

Jacob also erects a *matzevah* when he parts from Laban at Gal-Ed. That is, in addition to making a mound of stones as witness to his pact with Laban, Jacob "took a stone and set it up as a pillar (*matzevah*)" as additional witness (Genesis 31:45).

148

After leaving Laban, Jacob comes again to Bethel, the place where he had dreamt of the stairway to heaven; God again appears to him. God tells him, "You shall be called Jacob no more, but Israel shall be your name ... And Jacob set up a pillar (*matzevah*) at the site where [God] had spoken to him" (Genesis 35:10,14).

After the family leaves Bethel, Jacob's beloved wife Rachel dies giving birth to Benjamin, and the grieving Jacob sets up a pillar (*matzevah*) at Rachel's grave at Ephrath near Bethlehem (Genesis 35:20). Thus, the fourth pillar.

What makes these pillars particularly puzzling is that *matzevot*, or standing stones, have an almost completely negative image in the Bible. Deuteronomy 16:22 admonishes the Israelites not to "erect a stone pillar (*matzevah*); for such the Lord your God detests." Since the earlier patriarchs Abraham and Isaac did not set up *matzevot*, and since the attitude of the Bible toward *matzevot* is so unequivocally negative,* we must ask why Jacob is reported to have erected them, multiple times, and why in just those three places. The answer to this first question will emerge as we continue to disentangle the text.

Another puzzle about Jacob is his neurotic behavior toward Joseph and Benjamin, his two sons by Rachel. The favoritism he consistently exhibits to both of them is perhaps understandable, given his grief over the death of their mother, the wife he especially loved, but for all that it is still stunningly destructive. Indeed, as one who felt the murderous fury of his brother Esau as a result of Rebekah's favoring *him*, Jacob should have foreseen the violence and exile that would be visited on his favorite, Joseph! Jacob is inconsolable after Joseph's bloody coat is brought to him by his sons as false evidence that their brother—sold by them to Midianite

*In only one instance other than in the life of Jacob does a *matzevah* appear in a positive light. It is in the account of the ratification of the Sinai covenant, where we are told that Moses set up 12 *matzevot* at the foot of the mountain (Exodus 24:4). But even here it seems to be connected with Jacob (= Israel), for these *matzevot* are intended to correspond to the tribes of Israel, that is, to Jacob's 12 sons.

traders—had been torn apart by wild animals (plate 9, p. 85). Jacob's refusal to be comforted about Joseph's supposed death is, again, perhaps understandable, but it stands starkly in contrast to his almost perfunctory comment "Shimon is no more" (Genesis 42:36) when Simeon (Shimon) is kept as a hostage in Egypt until his brothers return with Benjamin. Jacob's inconsolable state has even more startling consequences: He is apparently willing to face possible starvation during a famine *and* let Simeon languish in a far-off Egyptian prison, rather than send Benjamin, Rachel's other son, with his brothers to Egypt on a mission of family rescue from the famine in Canaan. How can this be accounted for?

The third puzzle in Jacob's life story is that on his deathbed, he takes the unusual step of adopting Joseph's two sons, Manasseh and Ephraim (plate 10, p. 86). Genesis 48:1-12 describes this scene in which Jacob tells Joseph that the two boys "Ephraim and Manasseh [his grandsons] shall be mine no less than Reuben and Simeon [Jacob's own sons]." This may explain why the 12 tribes of Israel include two of Jacob's *grandsons*, but does it make sense in the context of the narrative in Genesis? What prepares us for this adoption; what has transpired that gives it meaning beyond that of a deathbed whim?

The New Jewish Publication Society (NJPS) translation attempts an answer by adding bracketed words to the text of Jacob's explanation in Genesis 48:7, so that it reads: "'I [do this because], when I was returning from Paddan, Rachel died, to my sorrow, while I was journeying in the land of Canaan, when still some distance short of Ephrath, and I buried her there on the road to Ephrath'—now Bethlehem."* The bracketed insertion expresses the thought, common among many exegetes, that Jacob's adoption of Ephraim and Manasseh was his way of honoring the haunting memory of Rachel. But the connection between that memory and the adoption, and thus the true sense of Genesis 48:7, remains unclear.

---

*Some translations omit the bracketed words.

A ll of these peculiarities and anomalies are resolved if we recognize the critical fact: *Jacob was responsible for Rachel's death—and he knew it!* Careful Bible readers have always known that Jacob unwittingly condemned his beloved Rachel to death. For when Jacob gathered his wives and children, his livestock and all of his household to leave Laban to return to Canaan, Rachel stole her father's household idols (*teraphim*), unbeknownst to Jacob. Laban pursued Jacob, caught up with the migrating clan and confronted Jacob concerning his leaving *and* the theft. Jacob, unaware that Rachel had taken the *teraphim*, was deeply offended by Laban's accusation. To underscore his innocence, he uttered to Laban the fateful condemnation: "Anyone with whom you find your gods shall not remain alive!" (Genesis 31:32).

Vows or oaths uttered in error or in ignorance are common in biblical literature; inexorably and irrespective of mitigating circumstances, they have their unintended effect.[3] The discerning reader thus knows that Rachel's life is forfeit, and the tension in the text concerns only when and under what circumstances she will die.

Jacob's condemnation of Rachel is unwitting ("Jacob, of course, did not know that Rachel had stolen them" [Genesis 31:32]) but fairly plain to the reader. But did Jacob know—or learn—that he had condemned his beloved wife to death? That he indeed came to know it can be inferred from, and even corroborated by, the text.

Before leaving the critical scene where Jacob parts from Laban, we need to examine a few more details. When Laban caught up with the departing Jacob and accused him of stealing the *teraphim*, Rachel was in her tent, where she had secreted the *teraphim* in a saddlebag on which she seated herself. During the search that Jacob invited him to make, Laban eventually reached Rachel's tent. She managed to avoid standing up and revealing the stolen idols, saying that she could not rise "for the period of women is upon me" (Genesis 31:35). So not only was Jacob ignorant of Rachel's theft, but Rachel was ignorant of Jacob's dramatic oath that whoever the *teraphim* were with should not live. She was in her tent when he spoke the fateful words, and no doubt the infant Joseph was with her, perhaps sitting at her feet as in Tiepolo's painting (plate 8, p. 84).* This will become quite important. Now let us turn to the next critical scene, the return to Bethel.

Jacob did not remain ignorant of Rachel's theft forever, though how he learned about it must be extracted from the text. Readers of Genesis, both ancient and modern, seem to have missed this crucial point, even though a few exegetes have come close to the truth lurking in the shadows of the text.

Jacob returned with his entire household to Bethel after departing from Laban. Genesis 35:1 recounts that God commanded this stop on Jacob's travels: "Arise, go up to Bethel and remain there; and build an altar there to the God who appeared to you when you were fleeing from your brother Esau."

The return to Bethel certainly required some preparation; Jacob and his entourage would have to be in a state of purity in order to revisit the hallowed site of Jacob's theophany where he erected his first *matzevah*. Jacob instructed his household and entourage: "Rid yourselves of the alien gods in your midst, purify yourselves, and change your clothes" (Genesis 35:2). To this end, the people "gave to Jacob all the alien gods that they had, and the rings that were in their ears, and Jacob buried them under the terebinth that was near Shechem" (Genesis 35:4). Suddenly Jacob must have known. *"All"* the foreign gods must have included the *teraphim*, the idols we know were in Rachel's possession. There, on the outskirts of Bethel, Rachel must have given them to Jacob, without hesitation, because she was unaware of Jacob's earlier oath before Laban.

Imagine that moment. Imagine the heart-stopping, life-changing effect it must have had on Jacob. There, on the outskirts of Bethel,

---

*That Joseph was very young and dependent on his mother can be inferred. First, Genesis 30:25 informs us that Jacob decided to leave Haran right after Joseph's birth. Jacob seems to have put the flocks through one or two breeding cycles before he actually departed (Genesis 30:31-43). Thus, Joseph may have been one or two years old, perhaps three. Moreover, in the scene *after* Gal-Ed, at Penuel, we are explicitly told that Joseph was with Rachel (Genesis 33:2).

in the very shadow of his first *matzevah*, the stone on which he had rested his head, Jacob discovers what we, the readers, have known all along: that he had unwittingly doomed his adored Rachel. What an unbearable agony for Jacob, and for the reader, who now knows, not simply that Rachel will die, but that Jacob also knows—and that he knows his oath was the agent of death.[4] Correlatively, what tragic, innocent ignorance for Rachel!

Mercifully, neither Jacob nor the reader is kept in this state of anticipatory mourning for very long. It is, indeed, in the very next scene, immediately upon leaving Bethel, that Rachel goes into labor and dies in childbirth. But her second son, Benjamin, lives.

It is clear now why of Jacob's 13 children, Benjamin's birth alone occurs at such a distance in the narrative from the clustered births of the other 12. The impact of this powerful tale would have been immeasurably diminished had Rachel died before the return to Bethel, where Jacob saw her relinquish her hidden *teraphim*, recognized his tragic error and learned that his oath was Rachel's death sentence. On the other hand, the narrative art apparently required that Rachel die as soon as possible after Jacob's recognition, to solidify the connection in the text between Bethel and Rachel's death and burial near Bethlehem.

It is not just the sequencing of the text that cements the linkage of these sites. It is the unusual *matzevot* themselves. Fokkelman notes that the various pillars erected by Jacob had different significances, some positive, some negative.[5] That is, the pillars at Bethel were unequivocally positive, for they represented the ladder of the dream, the theophany and the connection to God in the life of the patriarch. The pillar at Gal-Ed was essentially neutral, in that it represented Jacob's covenant of nonaggression with Laban before God. Finally, the pillar at Bethlehem was obviously negative, a monument to the prematurely deceased Rachel. Fokkelman's assessment focuses solely on the relationship of each *matzevah* to occurrences at its site; the *matzevot*, in this view, are vertical pointers, marking watershed events by memorializing God's presence at the site. Fokkelman does not consider the horizontal significance of the *matzevot*, as markers connecting different places and calling our attention to an extended drama, enacted in stages, at a number of key locations.

Consider again where the *matzevot* appear: Bethel, Gal-Ed, Bethlehem. They *do* have an intimate connection with one another, precisely with respect to the drama of Jacob and Rachel. For it was at Gal-Ed that Jacob inadvertently condemned Rachel, at Bethel that he discovered what he had done and at Bethlehem where the condemnation had its dreaded effect. The *matzevot* are not random monuments at all, and they are all of negative significance. For Jacob's *matzevot* are all part of the tragedy of Rachel's death and Jacob's part in it.

Jacob's neurotic and destructive attachment to Joseph and Benjamin, the children of his beloved Rachel who died so young, can now be understood more fully. Rachel's death has long been deemed sufficient (somewhat implausibly*) to explain Jacob's behavior. But now we know considerably more. When Jacob uttered his rash vow, Rachel was in her tent. Joseph, still a baby, was undoubtedly with her. Later, when Joseph's brothers showed Jacob Joseph's bloodied tunic after they cast him into a pit, might Jacob not have had yet another moment of pained realization, recalling that Joseph was in the tent with the *teraphim* when Jacob had said, "Anyone with whom you find your gods shall not remain alive"? That would surely have convinced Jacob not only that Joseph was indeed dead, but that he, Jacob, was as surely responsible for Joseph's death as he had been for Rachel's. Would that not now fully explain his utter refusal ever to be comforted for the loss of his son? The silent burden of guilt would have made comfort impossible. He had killed his beloved wife with his vow. Now he had killed her firstborn, his favorite.

---

*That is, he overprotected Joseph because Joseph lost his mother at such a young age. But Jacob's favoritism was actually destructive, placing Joseph in jeopardy from his brothers. Jacob must have been aware of this. Such illogical behavior must be due to something much deeper than the premature loss of Jacob's wife.

There is yet more: For though the text is not explicit on the timing of events between Gal-Ed and Bethlehem, it is possible that Rachel was already pregnant with Benjamin at Gal-Ed,* and that Jacob knew or suspected this. If so, Benjamin, like Joseph, had been in the tent with Rachel. With Rachel dead and Joseph presumed killed by the power of his rash vow, Jacob would naturally have assumed that Benjamin might also be under its spell. How then could he ever let him out of his sight? This fear that Benjamin too would die explains Jacob's refusal, even at risk of starvation, to allow Benjamin to leave him and journey with his brothers to Egypt. Joseph (in disguise) had told the brothers not to return seeking more food unless they brought Benjamin with them. But Jacob refused: "My son [Benjamin] must not go down with you" (Genesis 42:38). Only when their food was gone and the famine became severe, only after the brothers pleaded with him, saying that the man (not yet known to them as their brother Joseph) warned them, "Do not let me see your faces unless your brother [Benjamin] is with you" (Genesis 43:3), only after Judah pledged his own life as surety (Genesis 43:9), did Jacob relent. Only then did he let go of Benjamin so that the sons could free their brother Simeon, held hostage in Egypt, and return with food to Jacob in Canaan.

We have resolved the first two of the three puzzles with which we began this investigation—the meaning of the *matzevot* and Jacob's overprotection and fear for the lives of Joseph and Benjamin. The third puzzle, Jacob's deathbed adoption of Ephraim and Manasseh (plate 10, p. 86), can now be resolved as well.

When Joseph was born, Rachel expressed the wish for more children (Genesis 30:24): "May the Lord add (*yosef*) another son for me." As a result of Jacob's vow, those words turned into a ghoulish, literal prophecy; Rachel did indeed have *exactly* one more son, for in the birth of Benjamin she died. Having carried the burden of guilt

---

*Her statement to Laban that she was menstruating cannot be an objection to this point, for that statement was a subterfuge to prevent her father from finding the *teraphim* beneath her.

for Rachel's death all his life, Jacob, on his deathbed, would under-
standably look for ways to rectify his tragic carelessness with words.
One thing he could do would be to provide Rachel with the additional children he prevented her from having in her lifetime. The adoption of Ephraim and Manasseh, even if it did not literally give Rachel
more children, at least gave Jacob two more children from her.

This adoption explains Jacob's statement in Genesis 48:7: "'I [do
this because], when I was returning from Paddan, Rachel died, to
my sorrow, while I was journeying in the land of Canaan, when still
some distance short of Ephrath; and I buried her there on the road
to Ephrath'—now Bethlehem." This reference to Rachel's death had
seemed out of place in Genesis 48, almost disruptive in the midst
of Jacob's speech to Joseph.[6] Now we understand why it is there.

B ut what is the full meaning of this text? This is the final secret,
beckoning from the shadows of the text. Genesis 48:7 is translated: "When I was returning from Paddan, Rachel died, to my
sorrow [Hebrew: metah 'alai], while I was journeying in the land of
Canaan, when still some distance short of Ephrath." The context certainly supports the translation of the Hebrew words metah 'alai as simply "died to my sorrow." Indeed, a comparison with Numbers 6:9
would suggest that this verb-adverb combination means something
like "to die suddenly," and Genesis 48:7, therefore, might be understood as Jacob's describing how sudden, and thus how sorrowful, was
Rachel's death. But there are two other occurrences of the combination mwt 'al* in Genesis, and they suggest a quite different reading
of these words. Genesis 20:3 describes God's appearance to the

*Mwt is the Hebrew infinitive of the verb "to die," and metah is the third-person feminine
singular conjugation in the past tense ("she died"). It is standard practice to transliterate
infinitives in consonantal form, without vocalization. Thus, mwt represents the Hebrew
consonants mem, waw and taw, which together form the root of the verb "to die." 'Al is an
uncompleted preposition (functioning here as an adverbial phrase), the translation of
which is what is at issue here. 'Alai completes that preposition with the first-person,
singular pronoun.

Philistine ruler Abimelech in a dream, after Abimelech had brought Abraham's wife Sarah to his palace, in the mistaken belief that she was Abraham's sister. God said to the Philistine ruler, "You are to die because of the woman that you have taken, for she is a married woman." The Hebrew rendered as "die because of" is *met 'al*.*

Moreover, in the repetition of the wife-sister motif in Genesis 26:9, Isaac responds to Abimelech's indignant demand to know why Isaac represented Rebekah as his sister as follows: "Because I thought I might lose my life on account of her." The Hebrew rendered by "lose my life on account of her" is *'amut 'aleha*.** In other words, *mut 'al* means not only "to die suddenly" but also (and, in particular, in Genesis) "to die on account of" or "to die because of."

Genesis 48:7, that strange intrusion into the adoption scene, thus may be rendered as follows: "When I was returning from Paddan, Rachel died *on my account* while I was journeying in the land of Canaan, when still some distance short of Ephrath." Why was Jacob adopting Joseph's children and posthumously giving Rachel the additional children she never had? Because it was his fault! The final pathos in the life of Jacob is that he cannot die in peace until he can finally unburden himself of the guilt he has carried all these years. And he must unburden himself to Joseph, Rachel's firstborn.

The literary artistry is astonishing. For the truth is, Genesis 48:7 is equivocal, it is ambiguous, undoubtedly deliberately. Jacob, great as his need is to confess, cannot simply say to Joseph on his deathbed that he killed Joseph's mother. So he phrases his confession in a way that Joseph can well be expected to hear *metah 'alai* simply as "died suddenly" or "died to my sorrow," while Jacob actually intends the same phrase to convey his confession, that Rachel "died on my account." The exquisite ambiguity allows Jacob both to shed his burden before

---

Met is the second-person masculine singular, present conjugation. The preposition *'al* here is completed in the biblical text by the following word *ha-ishah*, "the woman."
**'Amut* is the first-person singular, future conjugation. *'Aleha* completes the preposition *'al* with the third-person feminine singular pronoun.

Joseph and to conceal it from Joseph at the same time. Only in this way can we fully understand the enigmatic language of Genesis 48:7. And only thus could Jacob finally go to the rest he never found in life. *Reprinted from* Bible Review, *June 1994.*

[1] Jan P. Fokkelman, *Narrative Art in Genesis* (Assen: Van Gorcum, 1975), p. 235.

[2] Fokkelman argues that this *matzevah* is intended to be a concrete "postfiguration of the theophany" at Bethel, an eternal vertical symbol of the connection to God first experienced by Jacob as the ladder in his dream. See *Narrative Art*, pp. 66-68.

[3] The rabbis later read this phenomenon into a biblical verse in Ecclesiastes (10:5), which they understood (more literally than they might have) as speaking of "an error which issues from a ruler." Although it is not the contextual meaning of the verse, it is true to the biblical mindset. According to this mindset, Jephthah must sacrifice his daughter to fulfill his vow: "If you deliver the Ammonites into my hands, then whatever comes out the door of my house to meet me on my safe return ... shall be the Lord's and shall be offered by me as a burnt offering" (Judges 11:30,31), and even Ahasuerus's misbegotten genocidal decree to permit the nations to "destroy, massacre and exterminate" the Jews cannot be revoked, but only counteracted (Esther 3:13, 8:8). The rabbis not only understood the biblical point of view here, but themselves subscribed to some version of it, at least to the extent that it appears as a motif in some legends in the Talmud and midrash (for example, Palestinian Talmud *Shabbat* 14d and Babylonian Talmud *Ketubot* 23a).

[4] In the second-century B.C.E. pseudepigraphic book of Jubilees, it is said that "they gave up the strange gods and that which was in their ears and which was on their necks, and the idols which Rachel stole from Laban her father she gave wholly to Jacob" (Jubilees 31:1-3). But the import of this statement seems to have eluded the author. Josephus relates that "while [Jacob] was purifying his company accordingly, he lit upon the gods of Laban, being unaware that Rachel had stolen them; these he hid in the ground beneath an oak" (*Antiquities of the Jews* 21.2-3). Again, however, the momentous implications of this, given Jacob's oath before Laban, are missed. Finally, Fokkelman (*Narrative Art*), commenting on the purification prior to revisiting Bethel, states in passing that the Jacob-God relationship "may no longer be clouded by the presence of *teraphim* and other foreign gods," and thus the household gods of Haran must suffer the humiliation of being put underground. How Jacob got the *teraphim*, and the effect that would have had on him, seems again to have been missed.

[5] Fokkelman, *Narrative Art*, p. 235.

[6] This much has been understood by some, but by no means all, commentators. Many understood the interpolation of 48:7 as an apology to Joseph for not burying Rachel in the ancestral tomb in Hebron, even as Jacob extracted an oath from Joseph that he would bury him there (see, for example, Rashi, Rashbam, ibn Ezra and Ramban). This explanation fails because Jacob's instructions to Joseph to bring his body back to Hebron were given in a previous conversation (recorded in chapter 47), and the present conversation concerned only Jacob's adoption of Ephraim and Manasseh.

V

RACHEL
AND LEAH

*Now Laban had two daughters; the name of the
older one was Leah, and the name of the younger
was Rachel. Leah had weak eyes; Rachel was
shapely and beautiful. Jacob loved Rachel.*

GENESIS 29:16-18

16

RACHEL AND LEAH

Sibling Tragedy or the Triumph of Piety and Compassion?

SAMUEL DRESNER

Familial tension in the Bible is typically sibling rivalry, rather than Oedipal conflict. We are hard put to find examples of a struggle between parents and children in Genesis, although the popularity of the Greek myth would lead us to expect to find this as the prototype for all family stress. Instead, Scripture offers us example after example of the rivalry of brothers—Isaac and Ishmael, Jacob and Esau, Joseph and his brothers.

And of sisters. Distressing though these episodes of sibling tension are, the most tragic example of sibling antagonism is between Rachel and Leah. For Rachel and Leah the jealousy of sisters is compounded by their being wives of the same husband, a practice so frowned upon that it was placed on the central list of forbidden sexual relations in Leviticus: "Do not marry a woman as a rival to her sister and uncover her nakedness in the other's lifetime" (Leviticus 18:18).[1] In view of this explicit prohibition, the question naturally

161

arises: How could Rachel and Leah's marriage to a single husband have occurred in the first place? While polygamy was permitted by biblical law, Jacob's marriage to Rachel and Leah was not simply polygamous but involved two *sisters* marrying the same husband. The biblical prohibition against this is unmistakable. How did Jewish tradition deal with it?

Several answers have been suggested: The proscription against such a marriage was not yet in effect when this liaison occurred, the giving of the Torah at Mt. Sinai having followed by many centuries the events of the story. This same reason is also used to explain how Abraham could have served his guests a meal of meat together with milk (Genesis 18:8), clearly contrary to the dietary laws expressed in Exodus 23:19. Although the rabbis assumed that the patriarchs observed all the laws of the Torah even before they were given at Mt. Sinai, some say that this applied only when the patriarchs resided in the land of Israel but not outside the land—such as in far-off Haran, where Jacob married both Leah and Rachel. Another suggestion is that there was divine sanction to violate the law in this particular case, because the progeny of these marriages would comprise the heads of the 12 tribes of Israel. Still another explanation: Because Leah and Rachel each feared that whichever of them did not marry Jacob would become the wife of his brother Esau, God decided to give them both to Jacob.[2]

Whatever the justification for the marriage of two sisters to the same man, it is clear that as co-wives they were in an untenable situation. After all, both loved the same man, both sought his love, both wished to be the mother of his children and both felt envy of the other. Thus, "when Rachel saw that she had borne Jacob no children, she became envious of her sister" (Genesis 30:1); for her part, Leah complained: "You have taken away my husband" (Genesis 30:15).

The dramatic development of the Rachel–Leah story reflects a divine pendulum, now swinging toward one sister, then toward the other. At first the movement is in the direction of Rachel, the young,

SUPERSTOCK

IT'S LOVE AT FIRST SIGHT when Jacob meets his cousin Rachel, the young, beautiful shepherdess. This painting by the Scottish artist William Dyce (1806-1864), Jacob and Rachel at the Well, *shows Jacob ardent and Rachel demure. Rachel has Jacob's love but wants to bear him children; Leah has given him children (seven of them) but yearns for his love. "Passion's exclusivity left no room for Leah," according to author Samuel Dresner, and "[Jacob] loved Rachel more than Leah" (Genesis 29:30). Yet perhaps it wasn't that simple: Some commentators consider Leah a model of piety, and Rachel's silence during Jacob's wedding night with Leah an example of her generosity and love for her sister.*

beautiful shepherdess whom Jacob meets at the well in Haran. After Jacob helps her water her flocks, he reveals to Rachel that he is her father's nephew. Rachel takes Jacob home with her, and her father, Laban, takes him in. The text informs us: "Now Laban had two daughters; the name of the older one was Leah, and the name of the younger was Rachel. Leah had weak eyes; Rachel was shapely and beautiful. Jacob loved Rachel" (Genesis 29:16-17). Jacob agrees to serve Laban for seven years in exchange for Rachel's hand, and he does so, "and they seemed to him but a few days because of his love for her" (Genesis 29:20).

But after seven years, on the very night set aside for the wedding of Jacob and Rachel, the pendulum swings toward Leah. Because of the custom of marrying off the elder sister first, Leah is substituted for Rachel on Jacob's wedding night. In the dark of the night, Laban brings Leah to Jacob, "and he cohabited with her," thinking she was Rachel (Genesis 29:23). In the morning, Jacob discovers the deceit: Outraged, he confronts Laban, and the pendulum swings back toward Rachel. Jacob insists that Laban give him Rachel as his other wife. Laban agrees to do so, after the first week of the marriage to Leah. In exchange, Jacob must work another seven years.

But it is Leah who is given an abundance of sons "because the Lord saw she was unloved" (Genesis 29:31), while Rachel remains barren. Rachel gives her maid Bilhah to Jacob so that "through her [Rachel] too may have children" (Genesis 30:3), and Bilhah bears two sons. But Leah's maid also bears sons, and Leah herself eventually bears more sons and a daughter.

Finally the pendulum rests with Rachel, whom God "remembered ... and opened her womb" (Genesis 30:22), so that she conceives and, at last, bears her first son, Joseph.

This fast-moving theater, in typical biblical style, is tightly condensed into the fewest possible verses—even more compressed in Hebrew than in translation—half concealing worlds of hope and despair that later writers expanded on endlessly.

The conflict between Rachel and Leah focuses on the contest between *love* and *motherhood*. Is there some scale of priority to choose between them? On the one hand, continuation of the covenant between God and his people requires children; on the other, true marriage demands love. Is succession so important that it can be

satisfied with the loveless creation of children? It would seem so,
for in despair of bearing children themselves, both Abraham's wife
Sarah and Jacob's wife Rachel present their respective husbands with
their maids to bear children in their stead. Conversely, can a childless love-marriage succeed? We hear no complaint from Jacob about
Rachel's barrenness in the years before she conceives. (Is it because
he had children through Leah?) But neither Rachel nor Leah was
satisfied with her lot. Each wanted both love *and* motherhood.

The struggle between them is nowhere given so clearly as in the
names the sister-wives—never the father—give to their natural and
surrogate children. In biblical days names were not given for their
caressing sound or endearing association, or even to carry on a family name, as is the custom today; rather, names were intended to
capture and convey the meaning of the life they denoted. At the
birth of each of Jacob's children, they are given a name by Rachel
or Leah, followed immediately in the text by an explanation of the
name. The explanation expands on the meaning of the Hebrew elements of the name. These names clearly express the motherhood-
love tension, with Rachel possessing Jacob's love but seeking motherhood, and Leah possessing motherhood but seeking Jacob's love.

Consider how the names, and the meanings of the names ascribed
to them by Leah, express her yearning for Jacob's love:

Reuben (Hebrew: ראובן, "see" + "son") = "See, God has given me a
son and surely now my husband will love me."

Simeon (Hebrew: שמעון, "to hear") = "The Lord heard that I was
unloved and has given me this one also."

Levi (Hebrew: לוי, "to join") = "Now will my husband be joined to
me, for I have borne him three sons."

Genesis 29:32-34

Leah already had Jacob as husband-father, but she wanted his
love as well. Herein lies the tragedy of Leah's life. For how was she
to gain that love? Can love be cajoled, commanded, produced by

165

publicity, called up on demand, summoned by fiat or tears—or through children? Must it not emerge of itself, if it is to emerge at all? And of that, there was little possibility in the shadow of Rachel, whose romance with Jacob was immediate and decisive, exceptional and persistent, and contrary to the then normal pattern whereby marriage preceded love. Jacob's love for Rachel was the love of passion, a mutual passion that is "necessarily exclusive."[3] What room, then, could there be for Leah? Was she not forced upon Jacob through intrigue by her father, who claimed to be bound by the custom of the land to marry the elder daughter first, and did she not cooperate in the scam, according to some rabbinic commentaries, lest she be compelled to wed the wicked Esau? She would not have Esau, as Jacob would not have her. The man she can have, she does not want; the man she wants she cannot have. (The same may be said for Jacob when Laban substitutes Leah for the beloved Rachel: The woman he can have, he does not want; the woman he wants he cannot have.)

What could Leah have reasonably expected from Laban's intrigue? One midrash turns the screw tighter by having her exacerbate Jacob's anger when he discovers the substitution. Leah is said to have rebutted Jacob's outrage by pointing out that when she impersonated her sister by deceptively responding to his call for Rachel in the darkness of the nuptial chamber, she was doing no more than Jacob himself had once done. For in the darkness of Isaac's blindness, Jacob had similarly impersonated his brother by deceptively responding to his father's call for Esau to receive the blessing: "He went to his father and said, 'Father.' And he said, 'Yes, which of my sons are you?' Jacob said to his father, 'I am Esau, your firstborn'" (Genesis 27:18-19).

Could Leah hope for love under those circumstances? True, Heaven took pity and granted her children when Rachel had none, and this must have stirred Jacob. But love? Not according to the underlying meaning of the names she gives her children. Jacob seems to have all but ignored Leah; not once does Jacob speak directly to her alone. During the years when Leah's children were being born, and he might have seemed most receptive, Jacob was toiling a second seven-year stretch for Rachel! When he mentions his wife in later years, when Leah alone is still alive, it is of Rachel that he always speaks. In these circumstances, Leah's dogged resolution, expressed in the names she continues to give her children, is remarkable. While the sages make much of Leah's "restraint," finding in it a piety of sorts, these names are as close to a protest as she comes. They point to Leah's perseverance, which is confirmed by Rachel's sharp reaction after the birth of Judah, Leah's fourth son:

> When Rachel saw that she had borne Jacob no children, she became envious of her sister, and Rachel said to Jacob, "Give me children, or I shall die." Jacob was incensed at Rachel, and said, "Can I take the place of God, who has denied you fruit of the womb?"
>
> Genesis 30:1-2

Rachel's brusque demand seems out of character, unless we see it as the outburst of a woman who could no longer restrain her pent-up frustration, heightened over years of watching one son after another born to Leah, while she had none. How could she be a wife, even if beloved, without being a mother? Perhaps the implicit rivalry of the sisters foretells the rivalry between Leah's sons and Rachel's son, Joseph, and later, in the land of Israel, between the tribes descended from the two matriarchs.

Jacob's sharp reply to Rachel's demand/complaint—"Can I take the place of God, who has denied you fruit of the womb?" (Genesis 30:2)—seems equally out of character. Why was he not more sympathetic, asks the midrash? Was she not his beloved wife, and was it not natural for her to want children after such a long and vexing wait? Quoting Isaiah—"I have given them, in My house and within My walls, a monument and a name better than sons and daughters" (Isaiah 56:5)—a later sage defends Jacob, arguing that his vexation was meant affectionately. What Jacob intended by his outburst was that, though he would have wished Rachel to be the mother of his sons, his love for Rachel was unconditional; he would love her even without children. As Elkanah would say to *his* barren wife Hannah many centuries later, "Am I not more devoted to you than ten sons?" (1 Samuel 1:8).

In contrast to the names of Leah's children, which signal her desire to win Jacob's love, the names of Rachel's children, the first two of which are born to Bilhah, her maid, point to her unrelenting drive for motherhood. Thus:

Dan (Hebrew: דן, "to vindicate") = "God has vindicated me and given me a son."

Naphtali (Hebrew: נפתלי, "to contest") = "I have waged a contest with my sister, and prevailed."

Genesis 30:6-7

In explaining the name Naphtali, Rachel herself reveals the protracted conflict with Leah. The tension between the sisters seems inescapable. For all Rachel's jubilation at the birth of her maid's children, her celebration has as hollow a ring as Sarah's might have when Ishmael was born to her maid Hagar. Though Rachel claims and names the boys as her own, just as she told Jacob she would when she charged him to "consort with [Bilhah], that she may bear on my knees and that through her I too may have children" (Genesis 30:3), these children were, after all, born not to her but to a surrogate, leaving her as much an *akara* (a barren woman) as before.

Rachel's joy in "prevailing" is, in any event, short-lived, for Leah, not to be outdone by her sister, follows suit only too quickly by using her maid Zilpah as surrogate. So Gad and Asher are born.

Then, unwilling to wait any longer, perhaps in remembrance of Jacob's grandmother Sarah who bore Isaac when "Abraham was one hundred years old" (Genesis 21:5), Rachel begs for mandrakes—a herb thought to increase fertility—and in exchange she permits Leah to return to Jacob's bed. Leah then bears Issachar and Zebulun, and with the naming of Zebulun (Hebrew: זבלון, "to exalt"), she lays claim to Jacob's affection yet again. The name is explained: "This time my husband will exalt me for I have given him six sons" (Genesis 30:20). As an encore, she gives birth to a daughter, Dinah.

Against Leah's own six sons and a daughter, plus her maid Zilpah's two sons, Rachel can count only two sons, and those by virtue of Bilhah, her maidservant! The odds weigh more and more heavily on the side of Leah. At this point in the story, when defeat has followed defeat and all hope seems lost, Rachel's deepest desire is at long last fulfilled with the birth of a child. Her words upon naming him must reflect her deepest feelings: "'God has taken away my disgrace.' So she named him Joseph [Hebrew: יוסף, 'to add'], which is to say, 'May the Lord give me another son'" (Genesis 30:23-24).

Motherhood is Rachel's consuming concern. The disgrace of her barrenness has been removed with the birth of this child. But the name she gives him does not express thankfulness for the child nor does it refer to her husband. Her mind's eye sees beyond this son to the next; this one is meant only to be a forerunner of the many she prays will follow. Rachel's reproach of barrenness is indeed gone, but the completion of her task as a mother is, in her eyes, only beginning.

The divine pendulum swings again between the sisters and comes to rest at last—in the direction of Rachel.

Contrary to the apparent intention of the story and Jacob's expressed preference for Rachel, some writers find Leah the more desirable of the sisters. Leah, who was healthy in body and whole in spirit, needed neither the mandrake for fertility nor her father Laban's idols for her religion. In addition, Leah's conversion to Jacob's religion has been seen as evidence of piety superior to that of Rachel. While both sisters took upon themselves the patriarchs' faith in the one God, Rachel's conversion was tainted by her need to convert in order to marry the promised Jacob; Leah's conversion had no such flaw.[4]

Another favorable view of Leah is that her "weak" eyes, far from being a sign of physical disability, were evidence of moral strength.

For just as the younger children (Rachel and Jacob) were destined to marry each other, so were the older children (Leah and Esau) meant for each other. Leah, well aware what marriage to the pagan Esau would mean, wept uncontrollably, thus damaging her eyes; though the marriage between Leah and Esau had been arranged by divine fiat, such was the fury, the passion and the piety of Leah's tears that the heavenly decree was annulled.[5]

Nor was Leah passive in her substitution for Rachel on Jacob's wedding night. For reasons of piety and not romance—aversion to Esau's evil and attraction to Jacob's goodness—she permitted herself a role in the deception. It was only necessary for the lamp of the bridal chamber to have been put out and for Jacob, whose wits had, in any case, been dulled through drinking long and late the night of the wedding feast, to have had his calls for "Rachel" answered by Leah. Not until the next day did Jacob awake to the deception. "When morning came, it was Leah!" (Genesis 29:25).[6]

In search of praise for Leah, one comes upon the tale of the miraculous exchange of embryos! A rabbinic extrapolation of the text tells us that Rachel's first pregnancy was not with Joseph but with Dinah (who was eventually born to Leah); Leah, on the other hand, was pregnant with Joseph, not Dinah! But Leah had divined that Jacob would ultimately be the father of 12 (male) heads of tribes. Were Leah to bear a son there would be room for only one more (her seven and two from each of the maids making 11). Leah—according to this retelling—felt it would be unjust to Rachel, even if Rachel succeeded in becoming the mother of Jacob's 12th son, to be inferior to the maids, each of whom had two sons. If this were to occur, Rachel would never achieve the status of a matriarch. How could Leah help her sister Rachel who had remained "silent" on that night that was to have been Rachel's long-awaited wedding night? Leah prayed to switch the unborn children (Joseph and Dinah) and by this act to repay Rachel for allowing the switching of the sisters on the wedding night. Thus Leah entreated that the fetuses be exchanged, one for the other. "And so it was ... *afterwards* [i.e., after Leah's prayers], she gave birth to a daughter and called her name Dinah [Hebrew: דִּינָה, 'Justice'] ... And God remembered Rachel ... and she gave birth to a son ... and called his name Joseph" (Genesis 30:22-24). Leah's entreaties were heard—Leah bore Dinah, and Rachel bore Joseph![7] Thus the substitution motif continues: from Jacob for Esau, and Leah for Rachel, to the unborn Joseph for Dinah.

Some of the mystics, as well, suggested the superiority of Leah, contending that Rachel represented the *alma d'itgalya*, the visible stage of the people Israel's task, the worldly and tangible aspect. Leah represented the *alma d'itkasya*, the invisible stage, the spiritual, recondite world. Leah's eyes, though "weak" in natural vision, were thought to have penetrated the mysteries. Taking these two stages as our platforms, the visible and invisible, it is possible to construct two periods in the patriarch Jacob's life: the first, when he is devoted to earthly, perceivable tasks, such as contending with the intrigues of Laban, gaining a livelihood, building a family and facing Esau, during which time Rachel was his mate; the second, after his physical conquests were completed, when his name was changed to Israel and his labors turned more to the invisible world, during which time Leah was his only wife, Rachel having died in childbirth. These two roles of the matriarchs—the worldly and the spiritual—are further suggested by their places of burial. Rachel was buried by an open road on the way to Ephrath (Genesis 35:19) that she might rise up to comfort the exiles who would one day pass by on their way to Babylon (Jeremiah 31:15), while Leah was laid to rest within the hidden recesses of the Cave of Machpelah, alongside Jacob/Israel and the other patriarchs (Abraham and Isaac) and matriarchs (Sarah and Rebekah) (Genesis 49:30-31).[8]

Whatever the merit of the arguments favoring Leah over Rachel, they cannot stand against contrary opinions provided by the widest range of Jewish and non-Jewish literature. The physical contrast

*TWO WAYS OF LIFE, the con-
templative life (Rachel) and the
active life (Leah), are represented in
Michelangelo's rendition of the biblical sisters. The marble sculptures are
part of the monumental facade of the
intended tomb of Pope Julius II in
Rome (see p. 177). Rachel (right),
in nun's garb, with hands clasped in
prayer and eyes raised toward heaven,
embodies piety, while earthy, stolid Leah
(opposite) symbolizes the vigorous life
of good works (such as bearing the
patriarch's children). But some Jewish
mystics saw matters the other way
around: Rachel represented the active
life, the visible stage of the people
Israel's task; Leah, the spiritual tasks
to which Jacob turned after the death
of his beloved Rachel.*

ALINARI/ART RESOURCE, NY

between the two, for example, is a favorite point of Christian writers.
Chauncey Depew observes:

> I have often wondered what must have been his emotions when
> on the morning of the eighth year [Jacob] awoke and found the
> homely, scrawny, bony Leah instead of the lovely and beautiful
> presence of his beloved Rachel.[9]

Nor should we be surprised that even so knowledgeable a scholar
as the poet Robert Browning, who knew the Bible in Hebrew, follows
the pattern, most commonly found in pictures of Jesus until the time
of Rembrandt, of favoring the Aryan "Rachel of the blue-eye and golden
hair" over the Semitic visage of "swarthy skinned" Leah.[10]

The Jewish sages observed that each sister knew the man for
whom she was destined, and, as the time of their betrothals drew
near, the more Leah heard about the wickedness of Esau, the more
her tears detracted from her appearance, while the more Rachel

ALINARI/ART RESOURCE, NY

heard about the virtues of Jacob, the more beautiful she became.[11] When Jacob first met Rachel at the well, he was so taken with her that he recited a blessing. For "upon seeing human creatures of unusual beauty, one should say, 'Blessed are You, O Lord, Who has such as these in Your world!' And there was none so fair as Rachel. It was for this that Jacob wanted to marry her."[12]

Other commentators have attempted to refute the arguments cited above in Leah's favor. So, for example, the suspicion cast on Rachel for carrying away Laban's idols for her own use is rejected in favor of the view that, even at the last moment of departure, she continued trying to wean her father away from idolatry. By stealing his *teraphim*, Rachel attempted to prevent him from enjoying his idol worship. Further, when Scripture says that Rachel was jealous of Leah, those who elevate Rachel explain that it was Leah's piety and not her fertility that she envied.

But the central event in Rachel's life that later writers focus on in a hundred different ways to laud her character is her quite remarkable silence at the time of Leah's substitution for herself in the marriage chamber—at the very moment when Rachel's dreams of marriage were to be consummated after seven long years of waiting. This restraint is regarded as one of Rachel's noblest features. As the Hasidic master Rabbi Levi Yitzhak of Berditchev tells it, "The merit of

[Rachel's] selflessness during the substitution of Leah for herself, lest her sister be put to shame, still succors us."[13]

Surely Rachel's decision to remain silent could not have been without anguish then or torment later. But in the brief space within which the tale is told—the more momentous the event the terser the biblical description—only the bare bones are given, with no hint as to Rachel's inner feelings. All the more reason for the masters of the midrash to dig them out. Thus, the name that Rachel gives to one of her maid's children, Naphtali ("to contest"), and the meaning she gives for the name—"I have waged a contest (*niphtalti*) with my sister" (Genesis 30:8)—is turned by the midrash into an *inner* grappling:

> I wrestled mightily with myself over my sister's plight. I had already perfumed the marital bed. Rightfully, I should have been the bride, and could have been, for had I sent a message to Jacob that he was being deceived would he not have abandoned her on the spot? But I thought to myself: If I am not worthy to build the world, let it be built by my sister.[14]

Another defense of Rachel: When Scripture says that "God remembered Rachel ... and opened her womb" (Genesis 30:22), the midrash takes it to mean that "God remembered that she was silent when Leah was placed in her stead." But was there not more to be remembered than her silence at the time of marriage? What of all the years *after* the wedding when she did not cry out? For she did not. And should you object that Scripture states quite the contrary— "Rachel envied her sister" (Genesis 30:1)—understand that it intends but to tell us that she envied the piety and the good deeds of her sister! This is the reason why there is no substance to the claim that Rachel did not deserve to have been rewarded with a child, because she was a sinner who violated the prohibition against a second sister marrying the same husband during her sister's lifetime. Scripture's justification in forbidding such a marriage, namely, to prevent sisters from becoming rivals (*tzarot*) (Leviticus 18:18), was not applicable to Rachel, since she was never jealous of her sister (except for her piety), either at the time of the marriage or later.[15]

For the mystics, too, despite their esteem for Leah, it is Rachel who is victorious. In good measure because of their veneration of Rachel's traditional gravesite, along the road to Bethlehem, that spot became, together with the Western Wall of the Temple and the Cave of Machpelah, one of the three holiest points of pilgrimage in the Holy Land. Rachel's compassion, explains the *Zohar*,* was such that she "achieved more than any of the patriarchs, for she stationed herself at the crossroads whensoever the world was in need." If Jeremiah turned the burial place of Rachel along the road to Bethlehem into a sepulchre from which she would arise to comfort the exiles on their way to Babylon a thousand years after her death (Jeremiah 31:15), the mystics transposed her gravesite into a station from which a merciful messenger would emerge from time to time through the centuries to bring solace and hope to the bereft. Indeed, they went so far as to give her name to the Shekinah, the Indwelling Presence of God, who accompanies the people Israel in their exiled wandering and shares in their suffering.[16]

Just as the exclusivity of Jacob's love for Rachel left no room for Leah during Rachel's lifetime, so after Rachel's death, Jacob's inconsolable mourning continues to eclipse Leah and banish her from the scene.** After Rachel dies, Leah bears no other children. Nor is Leah recorded among the consolers of Jacob after

---

*The *Zohar* is the classic work of Jewish mysticism.

**The Book of Jubilees, an apocryphal Jewish work, gives us a different picture of Jacob's relation to Leah: "And Leah his wife died in the fourth year of the second week of the forty-fifth jubilee, and he buried her in the double cave near Rebekah his mother, to the left of Sarah, his father's mother. And all her sons and his sons came to mourn over Leah his wife with him, and to comfort him regarding her ... For he loved her exceedingly after Rachel her sister died; for she was perfect and upright in all her ways and honored Jacob, and all the days that she lived with him he did not hear from her mouth a harsh word, for she was gentle and peaceable and upright and honorable. And he remembered all her deeds which she had done during her life, and he lamented her exceedingly; for he loved her with all his heart and with all his soul" (Jubilees 36:21-24).

Joseph's disappearance. Nor is Leah mentioned during Jacob's residence in Egypt. Nor are we told of her death. Indeed, nothing more is said of her, apart from two references in chronologies and a notice that she had been buried in the Cave of Machpelah.

A comparison of the sisters of another sort is found in Michelangelo's last sculpture, the great tomb of Pope Julius II. Pope Julius is depicted above a central statue of Moses with Leah and Rachel on either side of Moses, portraying, respectively, the active and contemplative life. Michelangelo followed the lead of Dante, who characterized the sisters this way.[17] To Moses' right, Michelangelo depicts Rachel dressed as a nun in prayer, symbolizing the contemplative life; to Moses' left is Leah, symbolizing the active life of good works (see photos, pp. 172 and 173). Though, according to the church, both ways are principal avenues in the service of God, it is clear which sister is being favored:

> The Rachel [statue] is the more expressive, elongated in prayer and "with her face and both her hands raised to heaven so that she seems to breathe love in every part," as [Michelangelo's biographer, Ascanio] Condivi wrote. Michelangelo clearly thought of her as a representation of faith. He spiritualized her in convent garb to the detriment of the stolid, earthy Leah.[18]

A final but unspoken argument for Rachel is delicately woven into the intrigues of the tale—an argument for monogamy. The struggle for a worthy family is central to the handing down of Israel's covenant with God: The creation of a worthy family is the primary function of the patriarchs and the matriarchs. The principal reason for avoidance of the Canaanites as marital partners was related to their sexual practices, as graphically spelled out in Leviticus 18. Monogamy was the marital ideal not only in the utopian society of the Garden of Eden with Adam and Eve, but also when Paradise ends and "history" begins with Abraham and Sarah, Isaac and Rebekah, and Jacob and Rachel.

THE TOMB OF POPE JULIUS II occupied Michelangelo and other artists,
off and on, from 1505 to 1545. The tomb was intended for St. Peter's in Rome,
where Julius was eventually interred, but the tomb itself is in the Church of San
Pietro in Vincoli in Rome. At bottom center sits Michelangelo's famous horned
Moses, flanked by Rachel and Leah. Whether Michelangelo considered the sisters
as rivals or complementary figures, he placed them in positions of honor, with
Rachel at Moses' right and Leah at his left.

177

Even the concubine-maidservants provided to Abraham by Sarah and to Jacob by Rachel when they could not conceive prove to be troublesome. The maidservants cause conflict in the marriages. When Sarah's maid Hagar became pregnant, "she despised her mistress"; Hagar's son, Ishmael, "was like a wild ass whose hand was against every man" (Genesis 16:4,12). Rachel's maid Bilhah had a liaison with Reuben, the eldest son of Leah, which led to his loss of the birthright. The maidservants prove to be stumbling blocks to monogamy, just as Leah herself is.

Indeed, Leah is the single exception to the monogamous pattern among the patriarchs. Her role is anomalous. She is a bearer of children, as were the maids, but she is also Jacob's legal wife, as was Rachel. The case of Leah, it could be argued, made a biblical argument for polygamy—except that the burden of the biblical story is the reverse; its purpose is to tell us that such an arrangement simply does not work.

Despite her legal standing, Leah knows that she is not recognized in Jacob's eyes as Rachel's equal. Despite Laban's scheme, Rachel's kindness and Leah's compliance, Jacob would not love Leah. He did not love Leah even after their children were born. His love was for Rachel, from first to last. Passion's exclusivity left no room for Leah. Leah appears as an outsider from the beginning. She is thrust upon Jacob by deceit, while Rachel is loved and chosen. Leah is fertile, conceiving (according to one sage) at the very first encounter, while Sarah, Rebekah and Rachel, to whom Leah is related (the grand-niece of one, the niece of the other and the sister of the third), were all initially barren. Furthermore, Leah's numerous children, described so harshly by Jacob on his deathbed, are the source of much misery: the brothers' kidnapping of Joseph; the firstborn Reuben's affair with Rachel's maid Bilhah (the mother of two of his stepbrothers), for which crime the birthright was taken from him and given to Judah; and Simeon and Levi's cruel slaughter of the Shechem clan after the defilement of their sister Dinah.

The separation between love and childbearing was common in antiquity. Polygamous societies accept a multiplicity of mates, while monogamous societies must contend more with adultery, prostitution and divorce. Leah and Rachel seem at first to serve the separate polygamous roles of maternity and affection. But neither is willing to settle for that; each demands both. Only Rachel, however, achieves it. The story reflects a kind of monogamy related to the bearing of children: The sisters do not bear at the same time; when Leah bears, Rachel is barren, and when Rachel's maid Bilhah bears, Leah is barren, and so on. It is as if something is wrong with both wives bearing at the same time.[19]

When the relationship between God and Israel is compared to that of a married couple, the human model is not that of fertile Leah–Jacob (blessed with children), but the passionate and faithful Rachel–Jacob, whose love is mutual and exclusive.

We have focused on the rivalry between Leah and Rachel. Let us end, however, by considering an intriguing commentary that reconciles the tension between the sisters and removes all bitterness from Jacob.

The Hasidic rabbi Levi Yitzhak reflects on Genesis 29:30: "He [Jacob] loved Rachel more than [or rather than] Leah."* While translations differ somewhat, they agree that Jacob favored Rachel over Leah. Levi Yitzhak, however, gives us quite a different reading: "He loved Rachel even more *because* of Leah." How does he defend this rendition, which is possible given the Hebrew words themselves?

> It is clear that while Jacob's purpose in working for Laban was to marry Rachel, Jacob, in fact, married Leah. But Rachel [by her silence] was actually responsible for this. Jacob's love for Rachel was then twofold: he loved her for herself, but he loved her even more because she brought him so pious a wife as Leah.[20]

Levi Yitzhak's vision turns the story on its head—no tension between sisters, no clash between motherhood and love, no anguish of a duped husband. All familial warfare vanishes. The matriarchs,

*The Hebrew is *va-ye-e-hav gam et rahel mi-leah*. The interpretation turns on the *mem* in *mi-leah*.

to him, are models demonstrating how to overcome family unhappiness through the power of love and the example of piety. Far from Rachel envying Leah, she was responsible for the marriage; and far from Jacob resenting the deception, his love for Rachel is only enhanced thereby. Human kindness and nobility of character conquer society's flaws. The tale is no longer, nor was it ever in Levi Yitzhak's view, one of sibling tragedy; it is the record of the trial and the victory of Leah's piety, Rachel's compassion, and Jacob's respect for the one and love for the other.

Reprinted from Bible Review, *April 1990.*

[1] Biblical quotations and verse citations are from the New Jewish Publication Society (NJPS) translation (Philadelphia: Jewish Publication Society, 1985). Where the phrasing in this chapter differs from the NJPS, the translation is the author's.

[2] Nahmanides, *Gur Arye*; *Tikuney Zohar* 40.

[3] Catherine Chalier, *Les Matriarches* (Paris: Cerf, 1986), p. 156.

[4] Moshe Teitelbaum, *Yismah Moshe* (Berlin: Pardes, 1928), vol. 1, pp. 75-76, *Parashat Vayetze*.

[5] Babylonian Talmud, *Baba Batra* 123a; *Genesis Rabbah*, ed. H. Freedman (London: Soncino, 1939), vol. 2, p. 653 (71:2).

[6] Freedman, *Genesis Rabbah*, vol. 2, p. 650 (70:19).

[7] *Torah Shlema*, ed. Menachem Kasher (New York: Shulsinger, 1951), vol. 5, p. 1198. When Dinah was born, the biblical text reads, "Afterwards, she bore a daughter," and not, as for all of Leah's other births, "she conceived and bore ... " The explanation for this change is that Leah did not conceive a daughter but a son. This is the force of "afterwards," understood to mean: "After she conceived a son, she bore a daughter." See *Torah Temima*, ed. Baruch Epstein (Tel Aviv: Am Olam, 1951), vol. 1, p. 279, to Genesis 30:21.

[8] Eliyahu Dessler, *Mikhtav me-Eliyahu* (Jerusalem, 1963).

[9] Chauncey Depew, "Woman," in *Champlin Orations*, vol. 4 (New York: 1910), p. 3.

[10] Robert Browning, *The Ring and the Book, Complete Works*, vol. 6 (New York: Sprowl, 1899), p. 72.

[11] Babylonian Talmud, *Baba Batra* 123a.

[12] *Midrash Tanhuma* on the verse in Genesis 29:10.

[13] Levi Yitzhak, *Kedushat Levi* (Jerusalem: 1958), p. 25b.

[14] *Genesis Rabbah* 71.

[15] *Genesis Rabbah* 73. *Genesis Rabbah* 71, *Ketav Sopher*.

[16] *Zohar*, vol. 1, pp. 168b, 225b; vol. 2, p. 29b.

[17]Dante, *Purgatorio* 27.103.

[18]H. Hibbard, *Michelangelo* (New York: Vendome, 1978), p. 174. While the *Zohar* sees Leah representing the "hidden world" and Rachel the "public world," Dante, and Michelangelo following him, portray them as the opposite, Leah as symbolizing the active life, and Rachel, the contemplative life.

[19]Chalier, *Les Matriarches*, p. 158.

[20]Yitzhak, *Kedushat Levi*, p. 53.